THE FREEDOM YEARS

THE FREEDOM YEARS

TACTICAL TIPS FOR
THE TRAILBLAZER GENERATION

Michael Shea

CAPSTONE

Published in 2006 by Capstone Publishing Ltd (A Wiley Company), The Atrium, Southern Gate Chichester, West Sussex, PO19 8SQ, England
Phone (+44) 1243 779777

Email (for orders and customer service enquires): cs-books@wiley.co.uk
Visit our Home Page on www.wiley.co.uk or www.wiley.com

Other Wiley Editorial Offices
John Wiley & Sons Inc., 111 River Street, Hoboken, NJ 07030, USA
Jossey-Bass, 989 Market Street, San Francisco, CA 94103-1741, USA
Wiley-VCH Verlag GmbH, Boschstr. 12, D-69469 Weinheim, Germany
John Wiley & Sons Australia Ltd, 42 McDougall Street, Milton, Queensland 4064, Australia
John Wiley & Sons (Asia) Pte Ltd, 2 Clementi Loop #02-01, Jin Xing Distripark, Singapore 129809
John Wiley & Sons Canada Ltd, 22 Worcester Road, Etobicoke, Ontario, Canada M9W 1L1

Library of Congress Cataloguing-in-Publication Data is available

British Library Cataloguing in Publication Data

A catalogue record for this book is available from the British Library

ISBN-13: 978-1-84112-688-3
ISBN-10: 1-84112-688-8

Typeset in 13 /16pt by Sparks, Oxford (www.sparks.co.uk)
Printed and bound in Great Britain by TJ International Ltd, Padstow, Cornwall
This book is printed on acid-free paper responsibly manufactured from sustainable forestry in which at least two trees are planted for each one used for paper production.
10 9 8 7 6 5 4 3 2 1

CONTENTS

ACKNOWLEDGEMENTS

I would like to thank my wife Mona, Ellen Grec Stensen, Malcolm Morgan, Norman and Maggie Hackett, Sir John Hall, and never forgetting the late Trevor Clarke, for all their lively advice and guidance. I would also like to acknowledge with gratitude the large numbers of members of audiences I have lectured to over the past few years on some of the subjects contained in this book. They have added anonymously but greatly to the store of ideas on constructive ageing. And finally my thanks also goes to my stimulating and challenging editor, Sally Smith.

FACTS AND FANTASIES: NOTE ON THE STATISTICS

A friend once remarked that he was now sixty-five years old, plus VAT. It all depends on how we look at figures. The statistics used in this book come either from United Nations publications or from British, American, and other national governmental statistical offices. As always, some statistics seem to conflict directly with each other: facts and figments blend easily together. Here they are used in very general terms only, to indicate how life expectancy for males and females has changed, and is still changing, with the greatest rapidity throughout large parts of the developed and developing world.

QUOTE, UNQUOTE

We may remember the famous story of Oscar Wilde regretting that he'd not made some particularly clever remark, to which his friend, James McNeill Whistler's response was, 'You will, Oscar, you will.' Quotations, anecdotes, and funny remarks about age and the elderly are legion. The majority of them tend to be attributed to certain people, very frequently to Oscar Wilde, George Bernard Shaw, Mark Twain and George Burns. A large number of them are mere variations or derivatives of even older sayings or stories. In several contemporary books of quotations, exactly the same anecdotes and caustic remarks can be found relaunched by different, usually youthful, comedians, who have rifled and adapted those great quotations from the past for their own audiences. And no harm in that.

TO DISGRACEFULLY MISQUOTE W B YEATS …

*'Before you're old and grey and full of sleep
And nodding by the fire, take down this book …'*

INTRODUCTION

'The time of life is short …
To spend that shortness basely were too long.'
    Shakespeare – Henry IV Part 2

Popular perception has it that vibrant, useful life starts fizzling out as we approach our sixties. That downturn is widely assumed to make us crash into the buffers on the very day we retire from the full-time rat race. At the outset of the twenty-first century, all those outdated ideas about age and the ageing process need to be junked in the proverbial dustbin of history.

The Freedom Years explains why we should ditch those geriatric myths. We need to scrap western society's institutionally widespread and decrepit attitudes to ageing. This is because the health and longevity of the populations of almost all the rich countries in the world have increased hugely in recent years and the pace is continuing to accelerate. It's a great human success story.

The clarion call of this book is for us all to work out a set of post-retirement tactics – free from compulsory work targets, free from crippling mortgages and other commitments, free from young families who have flown the nest. We have quit the so-called Sandwich Generation where we were stuck between ageing parents and adolescent children, and from lots of other past constraints. We still have continuing family and domestic duties to attend to, looking after our finances and maybe having some voluntary, pro bono responsibilities as well. But we're not required to work a forty-

or fifty-hour week any more, nor commute by car, bus or train, nor be at our desks by nine in the morning, nor attend board meetings and take conference calls, nor to go on long business trips. With the right attitude and determination we can also unshackle ourselves from the constant beck and call of our e-mails and mobile phones. *The Freedom Years* is what life can and should be all about from now on.

So why call us *The Trailblazer Generation*? Because, as part of this contemporary, world-wide *Age Quake*, we are way out in front of all other age groups, breaking new ground, charting new courses and finding new destinations and opportunities. We're not living by previous rules and clocks any more. Well armed with all the latest medical and surgical advances, we're breaking through many of the old walls and boundaries of age and ageing. We can afford to re-brand ourselves as being real Trailblazers whether we are baby boomers born just after the Second World War or whether we are of a generation a few years above or below them. Yes, in the past some outstanding individuals were there before us, living to a great and distinguished age. But they were very few in number in relation to the population of their times. We are a very much larger, more vital and increasingly healthy, wealthy, and experienced age group, that looks to a present and a future brim-full of exciting new possibilities.

The chapters that follow set out some of the issues that arise as we leave full-time employment behind us and enter The Freedom Years. They set out a web of tactics for improving our chances of living in a more liberated and effective manner and avoiding the many potholes on the way. If some of the arguments are presented in a light-hearted style, there's a lot of tough advice buried in here as well which will help us solve many of the practical problems we're all going to have to face.

In more detail, the book …

Underlines the exciting opportunities offered by the fact that most septuagenarians these days have far better health and prospects than fifty-year-olds had a mere half-century ago. In popular parlance, and playing around with numbers, that means that sixty-five is the new fifty-five; seventy the new sixty, and so on. All that gives us lots of exciting time-frame calculations to work on in all the spare time we're going to have in future.

Attacks, at the outset, the widespread institutional ageism which is given additional currency by the popular media. It asks by what modern law of nature we should all, stereotypically, be forced to retire at sixty, sixty-five, or earlier. It argues that enforced retirement is a criminal waste of wisdom, talent, and experience. In the years to come, and there are at last some hopeful signs of this happening, much more flexibility is going to have to be introduced, not just because western governments have started reacting in panic to the so-called pensions crisis by arbitrarily raising the retirement age.

Describes how important it is to avoid the sudden cut-off between the grind of work and the uncertainty of full-time leisure: the old-fashioned retirement rite-of-passage. In our late fifties and early sixties we've neither run out of time nor out of life choices. But we do have to learn how to switch gear. The book suggests alternative ways of cushioning that crucial process.

Offers some highly practical, but fun thoughts on using *The Freedom Years* to best effect: growing old gracefully, healthily, meaningfully, actively, and fully productively. It encourages us all to do what we want to do, like making a quantum leap, and using our well-honed skills to pick up a totally new career. We can all recharge ourselves at whatever age we've reached. If we haven't achieved our life's ambitions up till now, it is not too late to be what we once wanted to be.

Deals with a range of practical, mental and physical problems that arise in implementing those ambitions, which by no means just affect older age groups, like ... er ... er ... forgetfulness.

It's always better to know some of the questions than all of the answers. In any case there are never any definitive answers at the back of the book of life. A colleague who proffered much valuable advice when he read the first draft of this book asked whether it was intended as a commentary or a guide. The answer is that it's a bit of both. Life's a road show, so this can be thought of as a tactical map whose coordinates can help guide us as to which is the best route to take. It points out all the road works, twists and potholes on the way to the liberty motorway. As mixing metaphors can be fun, think of these new *Freedom Years* as a bit like wandering through a well-stocked supermarket: the aisles and shelves are stacked high with opportunities. It all depends what we want to take with us in our shopping trolley as we go on our way.

The Trailblazer Generation's increasingly prosperous and powerful position in society as a whole means that we all need to undertake a personal stock-check and adjust our tactics to handle the difference between full-time work and the so-called leisure that succeeds it. We still have several decades ahead of us. We have to set ourselves new ambitions and develop an active post-work strategy through further education or by finding ourselves totally new creative interests. Bridging that fundamental gap also means fighting hard to rid society of all the old shibboleths, the widespread ageist discrimination that still lingers and tries to hamper our achievement of new aims. We go well-armed into battle, since the health and wealth of *The Trailblazer Generation* underlines the growing importance of Grey Age Power and the Grey Vote in all western societies. We must all hang together or, most assuredly, we shall all hang separately was Benjamin Franklin's famous call to arms. Today we *Trailblazers* need to unite in a similar way.

There's another nasty little issue we all have to deal with. We tend to let ourselves down by concentrating too much on the past. We have to seize the day today, ditching a lot of nostalgia as we do so. It's now that matters, and *The Freedom Years* suggests lots of tactics for making life profitable, manageable, and enjoyable from now on. Some writers have called this period in our lives the 'Age of Integrity', or 'Maturity', or 'Discernment', or 'Enlightenment', or 'Tranquillity'. If we plan it right, it can be all of these things. And we now have the freedom to find ourselves as well. We have time to decide what we want, no matter where we started out in life. Experience needs to run counter to expectation to call it experience, something we all have learnt in the past. But in this play of ours there are many unexpected acts to come.

This book deliberately avoids discussing detailed medical conditions, such as Alzheimer's, nor the natural aches, pains, and infirmities which will surely come to plague us all in the course of time. There are lots of books in the marketplace on bodily health and also on financial health matters such as pensions. What this book does offer is some Verbal Viagra so that we don't let our personal and domestic habits lapse into a cluttered and careless old age. It consequently highlights some important practical issues: secure and comfortable homes and positive lifestyles create the bedrock without which it would be difficult, if not impossible, to underpin our exciting new ambitions.

There is one absolute fact in life: the fatter any rule book, the worse the message. Here there are no rules, only tactical tips and suggestions. We have for too long been programmed and disciplined by our careers, and abandoning the past 'hours of work' pattern can be a startlingly hard frontier to cross. We also have gone through life using only a small part of our total potential, so, with retirement from full-time work comes an excellent chance to change everything. This is also a travelogue for those of us who, since there's no way of stopping time, are growing older every day. The book draws no scientifically based, grand conclusions. But it does offer prospects of a far more exciting life ahead, when we, *The Trailblazer Generation,* will play an ever greater part in society, and for decades longer, than we do today. It's an inevitable and exciting prospect. Now is the beginning of everything.

There's an old Chinese curse 'May you live in interesting times'. No curses, only encouragement here. *The Freedom Years* is for the new middle-aged who are about to enter or are already living through this hugely invigorating sagehood of life. But for any of you who belong to an earlier age group, here's a warning: don't put this book down! You too are ageing at exactly the same numerical rate as us. You too have a shelf life. You too should be planning ahead. You too will have, to coin a new expression, to *regenerage* as you age. In no time at all you too will be living *The Freedom Years* to the full.

CHAPTER ONE

Prime Time Planning

'In life there are no second halves.'

– F. Scott Fitzgerald

Ageing is no spectator sport. We all take part. Yes, in purely temporal terms we all age at exactly the same rate, but our minds and bodies don't obediently follow suit. We may think we have a ringside seat as we watch others grow old around us, but we're right bang there in the centre of the action.

All life is temporary, but constant change is here to stay. So many very fundamental things have altered over the past few decades. For a start, life expectancy in the richer countries has increased enormously in the last century, most of that magnificent leap taking place since 1950. At fifty-five, sixty, sixty-five, seventy, or more, we, at the beginning of the twenty-first century, are benefiting hugely from the exciting medical and surgical advances of the past few decades. A mere half century ago, we would have expected to have been dowsed to near extinction either by retirement's bucket of cold water or cut down by the Great Reaper's scythe. But today *The Trailblazer Generation* is the new middle-aged, experiencing a vastly increased longevity and a regenerated lifestyle to go with it.

At a recent dinner party a male guest was challenged to guess a woman's age. He failed miserably. She looked forty but was actually rejoicing at the prospect of reaching sixty in a few days time, since she would then become eligible for free bus travel. But she bemoaned the fact that she would still not be allowed a free flu jab, which in Britain is only available to the over sixty-fives. Our late fifties and early sixties can be a bit like that: an unguessable in-between age in more ways than one. It comes as quite a shock to us to realize that we've reached the age we have, and we're not always sure how to handle it. What many of us tend to do therefore is to deal with life one day at a time. But it's much cleverer and far more fun to plan for the long years that lie ahead.

This isn't a rehearsal for life. *This is it*. Day on day, the age of fish and cheese we have stored in our refrigerator has to be checked for its sell-by date. But for the

wine in the cellar it's another matter entirely. It can, like us, improve greatly with age. We're all given only once chance at living, only one go. Each of us is alone in that game, born to follow our lives through to the end. With care we can still emerge as a great vintage.

Here's some excellent news. In this new twenty-first century, it's no longer three score years and ten we're aiming at; it's four score years and more. But even the most far-sighted members of *The Trailblazer Generation* often haven't a clue how to prepare for this increased longevity we have been offered, since we're all of us new here. As a result, far too many of our age group are inclined to drift or switch into neutral gear after we retire. And that can be highly destructive with so many potential years still ahead of us. Which is why we need a few of these tactical prompts to make ourselves think anew about the very exciting land-scape that's out there waiting. In the developed world, we of our generation have never existed before in the long history of the human race. With all the greatly improved health facilities and surgical remedies avail-able to us, we are exceptionally able not only to extend, but also to expand to a quite remarkable degree, these later decades of our lives.

NUMBER CRUNCHING

Before anything else, let's try to define what we mean

by old. We've probably always thought of someone as old, at any age, as a person a decade or two ahead of us. We need only look back as far as when our parents were roughly our age. From the perception of our youth we remember their care-worn faces and bodies as they progressed towards the end of their allotted life spans. Now, while similar perceptions are doubtless held by the youth of today, behind the mask of the years it's all becoming so very different. Do we really feel the way our parents looked? No and yes is probably the answer since ill-health is still the enemy of ageing, and death cannot fail to arrive one day. But on the other hand, with a little care and attention most of us are now able to slow quite dramatically the pace at which we're likely to pack it all in. More and more of us live decades longer and with more fulfilled existences than any of our forefathers. Look back once more to the nineteen-forties, fifties, or sixties, and we realize another fundamental truth. We tended to grow up later, marry later, have children later, than any previous generations. All this, along with those recent huge advances in medical backup, has had a ripple effect which has given us an enhanced statistical bank balance for these, our present and future years.

The other day, a friend proudly announced that this was the fortieth anniversary of his thirtieth birthday. Good for him. There's no cure for birthdays coming along every year. The more birthdays we have, the longer we live. But how many of us remember any of our early birthdays with the big zero at the end? A few perhaps. How well do we recall our tenth, twentieth, or thirtieth? We may vaguely remember our fortieth or fiftieth because of some agreeable festivity with a number of close friends. And sixty? Yes, as we age, there's a growing amount of family and peer pressure to celebrate the passing of our later years. And sixty has a special resonance, which is why there are so many age-old sayings about it, such as …

- Eternal youth means our lying about having reached sixty.
- The best years of our lives start with a bus pass.
- Almost sixty, but from which direction?
- Not pushing sixty, but we're clinging onto it for dear life.
- Some people reach their sixties several times over.
- Sixty is a good age, particularly if we're ten years older.

No birthday on its own is a big deal. Why? Because *our age is just a number*. It's what lies behind that number that matters. Yet numerical age seems to be obligatorily attached to anyone mentioned in the media these days. Take this one example. A press report about a traffic accident appeared in one of today's serious newspapers. It read as follows. *'An elderly man, Peter X, 58, was knocked down by a hit and run driver as he was crossing the main A9 road…'*

Elderly? Fifty-eight? Come off it! Get that pen and paper out at once and dash off a letter of complaint to the editor. Stories containing numbers like that force us to concentrate on what is or should be considered elderly or old at the beginning of the twenty-first century. Take the world of motor cars. There are modern vehicles and there are veterans, but in between there are the great classic models. The traditional saying that *Life begins at Forty* used jokingly to be interpreted as meaning that, at sixty, we were only twenty years old. A more relevant expression for those of us of this classic generation might be that *Life begins at sixty*. Remember Churchill's famous wartime speech, and he was a mere stripling of sixty-eight when he made it, 'This is not the end. It is not even the beginning of the end. But it is, perhaps, the end of the beginning.'

Not only do we need to redefine ourselves, we have to get society to do so too. So let's be precise here and now. *The Trailblazer Generation* includes all those from their late fifties or early sixties onwards for a full couple of decades more. Political correctness has already allowed middle age to be re-categorized as 'mid-life', and the popular media have made us more aware of our bodies and the effect of the passage of time on our outward appearance. So if we are today's OAPs, we are really reaching *Old Age Puberty*, and we might even claim with some justification that we could be coming up to our mid-life crisis round about now. That's why we need to insist that those who commentate on life issues must, from now on, define elderly, or old (with apologies to those of that age, who I hope don't mind

too much) as beginning at, let's say, eighty or more, and not a day before.

Continuing to try to define what is meant by 'old' also means that we have to take account of the fact that some of us seem to age far more prematurely than others. On that front, looks can be particularly deceptive. Time may be a great healer, but it's a pretty lousy beautician. We're consequently presumed to be young or old largely depending on the first impressions others gain of us: the apparent state of our health, our physical agility, our mannerisms and habits, our weight, our abundance or lack of hair, our skin texture, wrinkles, and so on.

Put it another way. Ask yourself this blunt question right now: *Do I feel my body is actually younger or older than I am?* Is that an odd query or not? Absolutely not, because there's an increasing amount of specialist interest in comparing our so-called biological age with our real age. Americans have long made much of this procedure, which involves a detailed health check, usually referred to as 'Real Age Measurement'. This is based on the universal finding that we do all age at quite remarkably different rates, depending not just on our genes, but on how we've looked after ourselves in the past. By monitoring and altering things like general fitness, cholesterol levels, blood pressure, body fat, smoking, alcohol consumption, and the degrees of stress to which each of us are subject, medical experts all believe that we can significantly extend or diminish our biological age by a quite remarkable number of years. A totally different bit of American research also seems to confirm that those of us who remain highly active for a decade or more after we reach our mid fifties are much more likely to live longer, healthier, more fulfilled, and financially secure lives. That's another reason why, soon after hitting our first half-century, we really do need to plan ahead.

What else should we be looking at in terms of defining age? To repeat, age is just a number. It is an elastic, relative concept. So how else can we try to define it? Who should decide how to categorize the generations, and why? Should it be a national governmental duty for example, since in most countries it is they who legislate as to when a state pension should be paid? We'll come back to that particular issue later. But it doesn't answer common parlance questions like when being 'over the hill' actually hits us. Are we over the crest when we feel we're picking up speed on an all downhill run? Then people used cynically to talk of a woman being of a 'certain age'. What does that now mean? One very practical answer is that we're considered old in most contemporary people's judgement if we reached maturity between the two World Wars of the twentieth century, or served in the second one, or did National

Service before it was abolished in the late 1950s. We're old to the young if we're Baby Boomers. We're old if we remember food rationing, or talk about the 'wireless' rather than the radio, or remember having to pick up the telephone receiver and wind a little handle to alert the manual operator that we wanted to make a call, or never saw a banana till 1948, or first saw television at the British Queen's coronation, or saw the Berlin Wall being built, or always thought that a Big Mac was a raincoat to keep us dry.

PUSHING THE BOUNDARIES

One answer to defining what is old is that there is little point in trying to be too pedantic about it. We all have constantly changing time horizons. It also depends how old we are when we consider what is old. In our early and middle years, being ancient was a far distant prospect. As twelve-year-old children we probably thought of a youth of fifteen as old, and for a large chunk of the world population today, particularly in developing countries, thirty is already extremely old. For a growing number of others, sixty is not at all old and people of fifty are considered quite young. It's like the term middle-aged, one definition of which is when our middle starts giving away our age as it slips down towards the floor. Or that broadness of mind and narrowness of waist change places. Or that middle age is when we should know better but keep on doing it. Fun and fancy? We may think we leave middle age behind us as Mother Nature is overtaken by Old Father Time, and that such light-hearted concepts are absurd, but in one recent poll, *twenty percent of those over seventy-five actually declared that they were still middle-aged!* Then again, the average person never thinks that they are … average.

Attempts to define age arise from what Shakespeare called the Seven Ages of Man: birth, youth, adolescence, adulthood, marriage, retirement, death. Some argue that people become adult only when they earn more than they spend, but on that count a few will never reach maturity. So there they all are: mankind's apparently enduring, ritual stages. But that sequential way of thinking automatically programmes us to react in outdated numerical ways. And that, to repeat, is no longer what ageing is all about. In no way does later life merely involve either an elevator automatically carrying us upward towards some heavenly upland plateau or degenerately downwards towards the grim valley of death. Yet here most of us are, still rut-stuck into thinking about going through later life just as the old stage-coaches took passengers from one post-house to the next. We look at our future as those old hags once did, sitting with their knitting, watching the tumbrels arriving at the guillotine.

In this twenty-first century we need to think of later life in a blindingly different way. As members of *The Trailblazer Generation* we have to bin those seven ages and think anew. Better to look, for example, at three simple 'hoods' that the dictionary defines as conditions or states of nature. After Childhood and Adulthood comes Sagehood, with the latter offering a whole range of novel benefits and possibilities. It's maybe even better to conceive of these three 'hoods' running in parallel, each separate yet linked. Each is available to learn from, and each benefits from the others. In our late fifites and early sixties we go through the portal into our sagehood either willingly or driven by forced retirement. Once we get there, we have to make sure we adapt our minds by leaving all our preformed mindsets behind us.

It's not always easy. We share our lives with too many people, most of whom may be much younger than us. They, in their shorter lives, have experienced very different ways of training, of living standards, of technology, of medical experiences, and, in consequence, have dramatically different agendas and ambitions. We, like them, have had to adjust to the many changes we have experienced in our own lifetimes. We cannot continue to live as we once did. Nor can we try to re-enter the old territories or 'hoods' of the past. It's nonsense to attempt to revert to former lifestyles. Try as hard as we can, we no longer sail in the mainstream, since contemporary society too often considers us as surplus to requirements. The overall solution to ageing, therefore, has to be to explore a totally fresh parallel state, packed with new lifestyles and conditions. Our life still remains a journey, but we're better off looking at it as if we're entering a new world, with new scenery, options, excitements and challenges.

Let's move on. One of the hardest things for us to do in life is to face up to the age we are. So let's begin right now by getting up and looking very hard in the mirror. What do we see? Let's test ourselves by asking this very simple question: *If, for some reason, we didn't know what age we were, judging from our looks, what age might we think we were?* Whatever our answer, we need all the Verbal Viagra contained here to stimulate ourselves to re-engage or *regenerage* as we age, pushing the new boundaries of our lives to the limit.

FACT FACING

Whatever our age, or whatever we feel is our real age, Old Father Time is always hanging about with his scythe waiting to harvest us. Some of us will get cut off short by him, not even being allowed the opportunity to say hello to our wrinkles. Growing old is a privilege, and dying is a mandatory part of everyone's life. The Thief of Time can be a bit like a bad host at a party, hurrying us through the years, not allowing us to meet enough interesting experiences and people on the way. All life's a stage, with us, the performers. This is our story, which has a plot that has run from *Once upon a time*, and which can, with that bit of extra effort, end with *and lived happily every after.* That's our aim.

Ruins are the skeletons of what once was. We are what we are now. Whatever our age, we needn't become ruins for a long time yet. If we've neglected our bodies and minds over the years, we may think that it's far too late to do anything about it. Wrong there too. Missed the bus on the route to old age? Don't worry. Here's another one coming along. We're all born more or less equal, but some of us get over it depending on what sort of lifestyles we adopted in the past. Or start adopting right now. As we're all being constantly reminded, exercise, and healthy eating and drinking patterns can have a huge effect whenever we start. Why? Because it's not age, but again that biological 'real age' factor, or *our fitness for our age* that holds the key.

HISTORY MATTERS

Arguing about the meaning of old and the defects of ageing has ancient roots. Cicero, in his essay, *De Senec-tute – On Ageing –* which he wrote at the age of sixty-two in 44 BC, and he was a remarkably old man for his time, described in strikingly modern terms how to age well. He pointed out that ageing was not some sort of illness but offered real opportunities for positive change. Jumping a millennium and a half onwards, we know that male life expectancy in the Middle Ages in England is believed to have been around thirty-three. By the middle of the nineteenth century that had risen to just over forty, so not a huge jump in years. By 1900, when statistics had become a bit more reliable, less than a quarter of the population reached the age of sixty-five both in Europe and the United States. Life expectancy was still around forty-seven years, with the length of a male's retirement averaging out at a single year.

With a few earlier exceptions, it was largely in the inter-war years of the twentieth century that efforts were concertedly made to discover ways of increasing longevity. A number of doctors on both sides of the Atlantic began to urge people to look after their bodies with much more care. Healthy living-style organizations became popular. Fashionable society began to acquire suntans, started patronizing saunas and Turkish baths, and took to dieting in a peculiar variety of ways. So what's new on the last front? Graceful ageing became a popular thing to aim for, with popular writers and the fitness experts of the day arguing that people could, with care, prolong their youthfulness by as much as a couple of decades. Rejuvenation became the new watchword.

With the exception of the old friendly societies which were formed to protect and provide for the ill and the elderly, the history of positive retirement practices is both thin and of relatively recent origin. That whole concept, at least as it affected the majority of the working population, has been a major subject of study for, at most, half a century. Retirement was a rare event for most manual workers as it still is in much of the developing world. An agreeable senescence was seldom reached because of disease, starvation or predation. Retirement only happened when an individual became physically incapable of working. That template of artisans and manual workers working for as long as they were able was determined by the simple fact that otherwise they would starve. Many of those who lived for more than a year after this climacteric were seen as pitiful survivors, particularly in a highly class-determined society where pensions, both private and state, were rare, except for certain individuals who had served their country in the armed forces. This made for additional huge inequalities, and for many generations, if you were of a low social class with little income, you were two and a half times more likely to die before sixty than if you were rich.

Even in this day and age, major differences in retirement experience, even in the developed world, still depend hugely on class, gender, and ethnicity. As a result, retirement is still, for many people, a most unpleasant stage in life's progression. It's seen as disruptive and disturbing, offering nothing but a future of insecurity, hardship and distress because of a loss of income, of individual identity, and all the problems of readjustment to a potentially empty life.

Whatever the differences in the figures we decide to rely on, the pattern is unquestionable. The ageing of populations is a worldwide phenomenon, not just in the developed world but also in much of Asia, though accurate statistics are often few and far between. All this is seen by many governments, and by society at large, as a disaster waiting to happen, with the elderly apparently set to become an ever greater drain on future scarce resources. A lot of this is total nonsense, and most dangers on this front could be easily dispersed. If, for example, governments had the guts to do away with statutory retirement ages, many people over sixty could and would voluntarily continue to pay their taxes and continue to make a valuable contribution to any nation's prosperity. Instead, backed by widespread and negative perceptions of our increased longevity, all this is commonly seen as an 'impending crisis' rather than being recognised as a massive triumph for the human race. Growing old ain't what it once was. Like air travel a mere two or three decades ago, it was once a luxury for the rich. But now, like cheap flights, life expectancy for a male at birth in Britain is currently averaging at around seventy-eight. Indeed, if we're already sixty-five we can statistically look forward to living to eighty-five, and if we're particularly healthy and comfortably off, that can even stretch to ninety. Thus the countdown to a few very brief years of retirement is no more.

THE MARCH OF THE METHUSELAHS

Despite all the figures, an opinion poll in Britain in the middle of 2005 found that the vast majority of people simply did not believe that they were going to live any longer than their parents. To be persuaded to any cause relating to the prospects of greater longevity, examples of success have to be paraded before any such sceptical audience. And to the readership of this book. So let's roll out some names from history of famous people who reached a ripe old age, and who continued to contribute greatly to the progress of civilisation. OK, the Book of Moses says that Methuselah lived to the ripe old age of nine hundred and sixty-nine years. Or was that an early statistical nonsense and he really only made it to ninety-six point nine? The answer always lies in numbers. The ancients we are going to mention were very few in comparison with the majority of their contemporaries. We of *The Trailblazer Generation* are legion.

We've reached three score, plus five, and ten, and twenty, and thirty. There are a rapidly growing number of us around, though still relatively few of us die past a hundred. We all know more and more people in their late eighties or early nineties, who, as they approach their centennial, are still full of life, spry and sharp as pins. Several weeks spent recently with five hundred pensioners on a cruise ship, most of them over seventy-five, left a marked impression of the intellectual and physical vigour, enthusiasm and curiosity they displayed. The ones who really impressed were those who, sometimes despite serious disabilities or health problems, looked alert, dressed smartly, and remained challenging and bold. One wheelchair-bound veteran of ninety was, and is, among the most exciting people we've ever come across. Interestingly, ten of the others were also over ninety and were as intellectually sprightly as those years younger than them. Others, and sadly there were more than a few of them too, while still full of physical life, had failed to dig themselves out of the torpor of their ways, and had become anachronistic vegetables before their time.

Today's *Trailblazer Generation* includes more and more individuals who continue to sparkle on the world stage. Though the historical examples that follow are all of talented celebrities who stayed long in the spotlight for one reason or another, nowadays there are thousands and thousands of others who continue to break new ground, even though their careers may fail to hit the headlines as they did when they were in full-time employment. There are long lists of the great, the good, and the golden in all the western democracies: former politicians, captains and kings of industry, leaders of the professions, public service and the arts, who continue to give huge, often voluntary, support to many aspects of society from behind the scenes. In this book, however, such contemporary names are deliberately few in number since the Great Reaper may come along in the meantime to wipe their slate clean, and, in any case, the requirement here is to provide examples that are known to a wide audience. As always it is the general principle that counts.

If we're feeling a fraction elderly this morning, let's take a moment and look back across the centuries at famous examples which will mean something to most of us. In much less healthy times, when most men failed even to reach their forties, Michelangelo was still working on the decoration of St Peter's Basilica in Rome until his death at the age of eighty-nine. The great Titian was still painting with 'incomparable steadiness of hand' until he was cut off by the plague at the age of ninety-nine. Matisse kept painting right up until his death in 1954, at the age of eighty-five, while Monet didn't even start painting his water-lilies until he was seventy-six. And how about Pablo Picasso, or that great American painter, Grandma Moses, who was still painting at one hundred? In architecture, Frank Lloyd Wright designed the Guggenheim Museum in New York when he was ninety, and in literature, Goethe actually wrote his *Faust* when he was in his eighties, while George Bernard Shaw was still actively writing both books and journalism when he was ninety-three.

A few musical examples are useful too. Verdi composed *Falstaff*, widely considered to be one of the wittiest and best of all his operas, when he was seventy-nine, and Arthur Rubinstein gave a concert in the Carnegie Hall in New York when he was ninety. One of the greatest musicians of the age, Pablo Casals, was also giving regular concerts at eighty-eight. Indeed, when asked two or three years after that, why he still practised every day, Casals replied that he was still trying to improve his performance, and that led on to him conducting a United Nations concert including one of his compositions when he was at the grand age of ninety-five. Finally, Pierre Monteux was invited to become the Principal Conductor of the London Symphony Orchestra when he was eighty-six. He accepted, but reputedly insisted that they gave him a twenty-five-year contract with an option to renew!

There are several political greats who survived to a considerable age across recent centuries. Benjamin Franklin helped frame the American Constitution at the age of eighty, while Gladstone was still British Prime Minister at eighty-three. Can we imagine that happening now? Why not? Germany's first post-war Chancellor, Konrad Adenauer, only took up office in 1949 when he was already seventy-three, and served on, known as *Der Alte* – the Old One – for the next fourteen years. Even Mahatma Ghandi did not begin his major public campaign for Indian independence until he was in his early seventies. And what about Nelson Mandela's career after his long and terrible years in prison? In his late eighties (he turned eighty-seven in 2005) he is still a voice to be reckoned with all over the world. At time of writing, eighty-four-year-old Judge John Paul Stevens is showing no signs whatsoever of slowing down in the US Supreme Court. Simon Peres, at eighty-one, the veteran leader of the Israeli Labour Party is out in front as the voice of reason in that politically fractured country. And then there's Cuba's Fidel Castro who's rapidly approaching eighty … How many US presidents has he seen come and go?

The British Queen continues to hit the headlines on a daily basis though she is now entering her eighties. Accompanied by the Duke of Edinburgh, himself a full five years ahead of her, she has a very full work programme and still travels widely around the United Kingdom and overseas, representing Britain and the fifteen other countries of which she is Head of State. Back in 1952, her first prime minister was Winston Churchill, and the first US president she had dealings with was Roosevelt, men probably no contemporary politician ever saw, met or knew. The Queen also undertakes huge numbers of other high profile events such as state visits or opening the British parliament, when she has to read out a speech to several hundred political movers and shakers in the Palace of Westminster. She goes there wearing a crown and some very heavy robes. Prince Philip, a distinguished war veteran, wears full dress naval uniform. She won't abdicate. Neither of them is ever going to retire.

We could parade lots more names. For example, one of history's great heroes, Albert Schweitzer, ran his leper hospital in West Africa until his death at ninety. We will all have other personal examples of known and unknown people who have remained active and creative well into their nineties. Then there are the showbiz names that crop up again and again in the celebrity-fixated media like that great veteran in his eighties, Eric Sykes, who says that people keep coming up to him and saying that they thought he was dead. Think too of Elizabeth Taylor. We remember her in her youth. Now, after eight marriages to seven husbands, and, lately, skin cancer, a brain tumour, alcoholism, a crippling bone disease, how she has sparkled with talent and diamonds across the years. Incidentally, according to a study of seventy-two years of the American Academy Awards, Oscar-winning actors and actresses apparently live, on average, four years longer than unsuccessful nominees. Some Americans apparently call this the Winston Churchill effect. Success breeds success in temporal terms too, or so it seems. Churchill, as always, is a great example. He lived life to the full, smoked and drank heavily, was hugely successful in politics and as a war leader, but then changed profession and hit the headlines with his writing and painting, and lived till he was ninety.

In the United States, where they have for some time been holding something called *Age Quake Discussions* on 'meaningful ageing', senior citizens like Alan Greenspan, former Chairman of the Federal Reserve Bank, the Australian born Rupert Murdoch, and Warren Buffet, the financial guru, are all still highly active, yet they are well into their mid to late seventies. As one final example, Anthony Smith, the travel writer, also in his late seventies, recently advertised in London's *Daily Telegraph* for crew members who must be over sixty-five, to join him in an expedition sailing a raft across the Atlantic from the Canaries to the Bahamas. His mission: to prove that one is only as old as one feels.

Nowadays there are far too few people over sixty-five who remain key figures in any western country. Behind the scenes, however, many well known names from the past, despite their age, continue working. Their contribution to charitable work, to the arts and other endeavours, is immeasurable. But why are not more of them still hitting the headlines? Is it all to do with the tradition of ageism, particularly in the youth-obsessed media, where age is seen to be an encumbrance in any public or private sector organization? We will return with a vengeance to that question and to the one of marshalling 'Grey Power', later in this book.

We have yet to become a world where *The Trailblazer Generation* remains the powerful old. On the other hand, our ever-ageing population is not, as some commentators keep trying to suggest, an apocalypse waiting to hit civilization. Our increased longevity is, by contrast, a great triumph for all civilized societies. The new middle-aged now outnumber those currently in the working population, and when we are allowed to do so, we bring our prosperity with us. The Grey Pound has grown increasingly strong, and what Americans call *The Third Age* holds up to eighty percent of the West's disposable income, with, as one up-to-date example, Britain's over-fifties reputed to be the wealthiest in all Europe, their assets having increased by well over a third in the last decade alone.

MORE GOOD NEWS

So hang out more flags! This is quite definitely The Prime Time for Living. We are becoming a more powerful group within nations, increasingly active and forceful, tempered by time and experience, as those half our age. As long-term empty-nesters, we have more money to spend on keeping the economy going, buying financial services and spending huge amounts on the travel and leisure industries. Despite this latent financial power, many of our special requirements are still largely ignored, though there are an increasing number of businesses that are beginning to fill that gap. Youthful commentators of course laugh at the so-called Saga Generation, named after the highly successful British company of the same name. (Saga, they say equals 'Sex and Games for the Aged', 'Send Aged Grannies Abroad' or 'Sex for Sexagenarians'.) More seriously, the media in all western countries tend to reflect their governments' concerns over how much of a burden on the state, and particularly on pensions and health services, the elderly are going to become in the decades ahead. So maybe we'd better be a little careful not to trumpet our sumptuous wealth too much, for, quite apart from inheritance tax, governments might find other ways of taking more from us in the meantime. By the way, on the financial front, we're told that on the black market in Brighton these days, disabled parking badges change hands for up to a thousand pounds a time. There's a nice little earner!

Now is the moment to ask ourselves: if we dropped dead today, is this where we'd really want to be? Excuses, excuses? We don't have them any more. We probably have between forty and eighty hours per week – counting former commuting time – extra, liberated time suddenly available to do all the things we've long said we wanted to do, or privately dreaded we had to do. Travel the world? Yes. Take the spouse (how unpleasant that word is) on a long holiday without feeling guilty or worrying about going back to an office desk piled high with problems waiting for us on our return. Then what about painting the kitchen, replanting the garden, mending the fence, taking more exercise, though, as regards the latter, some cynics merely argue that taking exercise only means that we die healthier?

Adjustment to all this free time can be far from easy. It's exciting. It can be terrifying too.

In the chapters that follow we will look at many of the opportunities and some of the drawbacks to handling our advancing years. Enjoying our new liberty is the *sine qua non*. If necessary we need to get our doctor to prescribe us some of those happiness pills which, according to the tabloid press, only the young take when they get depressed. Not just Viagra and chips; Prozac and chips too!

Though we probably lack many of their outstanding talents, those examples of great people from the past should encourage us to continue a proactive life well into our late age. We are all time travellers. They were few, but we are many. Let's all use our *Freedom Years* to best advantage, benefiting both ourselves and those around us.

CHAPTER TWO

Lies, Damn Lies, and Statistics

'Few people know how to be old.'
                              – La Rochefoucauld

British railway companies announced recently that they were adding minutes to many journeys in their timetables 'to avoid the public quoting unfortunate statistics about trains running late'. That's about as daft as one can get, but some numbers are important: we need to understand them and get them into perspective. Disraeli said that there are three kinds: lies, damn lies, and statistics. We are about to look at some recent ones on future longevity, and though we should always treat them with some suspicion, the trends are certainties. Before we get on to that, however, let's briefly put things in context. Let's have a first glance at *The Freedom Years* ahead of us and decide how we're going to go about filling them.

Carpe Diem! 'Seize the day' always sounds a bit like advocating jumping on whichever is the first of those trains to come along. It may be the wrong train, on the wrong route, on the wrong day. We need to study life's timetable, however oddly it's manipulated, and decide where and when we're going from now on, and what baggage we want to take with us. Different people see that journey across the years in very different ways: as a pleasant amble, as a race, as a stimulating challenge or, sadly, as a constant and unpleasant battle. To change the whole transportation metaphor, we are the pilots of our own future. It's up to us to handle the controls and get onto the right flight path. There's still a lot of exciting bright blue sky up there.

As background to the statistics that are about to amaze us, there are so very many liberating freedoms now available to us. No employer is controlling our lives now. There's no one else to blame for any problems we have, and it's up to us to decide what we do next. We don't need to worry any more about what people think about us. In any case, as we grow older, we realize how little they do think about us in any event. In our new, enlightened age, we can handle disappointments much more easily, realising that frequently in the past we set our expectations too high in any event. We stop making promises we can't keep, but we still have a lot of unfinished business to attend to.

Some facts are irrefutable, but it all depends on how we look at them. Do rose bushes have thorns? Do thorn bushes have roses? Choose your own interpretation. We pass through life only once, and we won't come this way again. Whatever our perspective, the past can't be changed. But the future still can. Banal though it may sound, the rest of our life begins today, whatever age we are. Today, any day, is when the past, present and future come together. Each day can become a miniature lifetime, and one of the most difficult questions is not just how to cope with it, but how to benefit from it as well. So many of us spend so much time putting out today's fires that we forget to plan for what can be a long run ahead.

The fundamental questions we should be asking ourselves are:

- Are we really going to live such healthier, longer lives? If so …
- What are our hopes and aspirations for the years ahead?
- What are we particularly looking forward to?
- What hindrances do we expect to waylay our plans?
- What other worries lurk in the undergrowth?

Time becomes more and more important when there's less and less left of it. Yet with all those exciting super-tomorrows ahead, this stage in life-living becomes a Renaissance, an encore to our careers so far. We need to make ourselves age-proof to cope with it. We need to construct a new vision for ourselves, one of self-reliance, continued engagement, and reinvention rather than uneventful inactivity. We need to be venturesome, keep circulating, take some risks, experiment, and find a deeper purpose for the rest of our lives. Why? Because, as a Harvard University report recently pointed out (May, 2005), sitting around doing nothing seriously shortens lives. We all have our skills. It is the future management of them and not neglecting them that matters. If we do that we can find a new energy, and increase our capabilities, particularly when challenges or emergencies arise. Think of that seventy-year-old grandmother who recently knocked out a burglar with a garden gnome or the ninety-four-year-old who completed the Edinburgh Marathon in June 2005.

THE WORLD WIDE WEB

A famous philosopher once remarked that life is a sexually transmitted disease, and the mortality rate is one hundred percent. That's a great but levelling statistic to start off with. It backs up the challenges set out above. There are lots and lots of national and international statistics on ageing floating around. Someone once said that forty-two point five percent of them are made up by politicians to reinforce their policies on pensions. Good figures can easily be turned into unreliable ones. Statistics don't always lie, but often don't stand up either. Experts in particular warn that predicting the demographics of the twenty-first century is a very inexact science, given the unexpected and unknown with regards to birth rates, AIDS, and many other as yet to be discovered health and environmental problems.

Here's a fresh statistic for starters. It is widely reported that the whole planet is greying, which means that each month another million or so people turn sixty. Of course there are huge differentials in life-expectancy figures in different parts of the world, with some Asian countries catching up fast with the western world, but Africa lingering a desperately long way behind, and likely to remain so for many decades to come. A recent UN report questions the whole business of guesstimating future longevity levels. Far too much is unknown. All we need, they go on to say, is something like a world-wide bird flu pandemic to fill the graveyards and turn such statistics into ash. On the positive side they also admit that we can't even begin to guess at what exciting future medical revolutions may emerge. The same report sensibly goes on to wonder what the number of heart and kidney transplants, or hip replacements, of the twenty-first century might be which could transform so very many lives. It doesn't attempt to give any answers. We of the *Trailblazer Generation* ought to understand all this: many of us alive today remember our pasts without a motor car, a washing machine, inside toilets, or even electricity. We need to look only a little bit back in life to begin to understand what else might lie ahead. We had absolutely no concept in our youth of modern technology, from the personal computer to the mobile phone. And as for a heart transplant? 'You must be joking!' even a medical specialist in the first half of the twentieth century would have protested.

LONGEVITY LIVES!

Once upon a time people had to learn how to grow up, but nowadays, with our extended life spans, we have to learn how to grow old. If we are Darwinians, we know that the earliest human beings only lived long enough to ensure that their offspring could breed and the species could survive. Things have moved on a bit since then. We have to pick and choose our numbers, but current presumptions are generally agreed. Here are some to play with.

According to UK demographic statistics, if we were born in Britain in the first decade of the twentieth century, our average life expectancy, as a man, was still well under fifty years of age. By 1951 that figure had risen to fifty-eight for men and sixty-two for women. Throughout all of Western Europe the twentieth century added at least twenty-five years to the average life span. Now, at the beginning of the twenty-first century, in most of the western world, both genders can hope to add around twenty more highly stimulating years to those figures.

If we are currently aged fifty, we are lucky: only five percent of our age group, male and female, are already dead. By the age of seventy-five, however, fifty percent of European men have turned to dust. That little statistic may remind us of Tom Lehrer's remark that 'by the time Mozart was my age, he'd been dead for ten years.'

In the US and Canada, because age-care is generally a bit more advanced than in much of Europe, we can add another year or two to these life expectancy figures. Despite that, there are, throughout all of North America, huge discrepancies depending on our gender, our ethnicity, and where and how we live or have lived our lives.

This means that in most of the richer world, there are already slightly more non-workers than workers, a figure that is estimated to rise dramatically to around three non-workers for every worker by the year 2030. All of which partially explains why governments are getting so worried about future pension pots and health costs.

In Japan it is now predicted that by that same year, a quarter of the population will be over sixty-five, and the number of over-eighties is expected to treble. Some UN figures, despite their many caveats, go on to suggest that by 2040 the leap will be even more telling, with fifty percent of the world's population being over seventy-five.

Currently, there are around six thousand people in Britain over one hundred years old. That figure is increasing by seven percent per annum, which is putting a lot of strain on the resources of Buckingham Palace in sending out birthday greetings to these centenarians from the Queen. On average throughout all the other prosperous western countries, the number of centenarians has doubled in every single decade since the middle of the last century. As another odder statistic on this front, while in Japan back in 1963 they listed a mere one hundred and fifty-four centenarians, today there are twenty-three thousand of them!

All this means, incidentally – and a friend remembers his mother saying one morning that she couldn't possibly have a son who was sixty – that we in the western world can now perfectly easily have two generations of so-called retirees in the same family.

GENDER BENDING

The clock of time is only wound up once, proclaims the old saying. Come to think of it, however, we could argue that, though time never stops, its clock can be wound up again when we're half way through. Leaving that aside for now, let's get some more life-expectancy facts up on the blackboard. Professional demographers, please don't quibble. It's the general tendency we're after. (Odd Fact for them to ponder over: When people fill in application forms to take out life insurance for themselves, in answer to a question that relates to their genetic background, 'What did your parents die of?' a large number of applicants write, 'Nothing serious'.)

The much debated longevity ratio, men to women, is also changing. In the past, being a mere man was the death of us. We automatically popped our clogs a considerable number of years earlier than our female partners. That is still largely the case, but let's look at some changing, and truthful, statistics on this particular front.

FACT: Currently, in the western world male life expectancy still lags some seven years behind females. That can hit us hard when, as we grow older, we note the strong gender imbalance as we cross off names in our address books.

FACT: This gender differential is held to be because the Y chromosome kills sooner, of heart attacks, cancer, strokes, or whatever. One emerging medical theory about the difference in life spans between the male and the female concentrates on the strength of their hearts. Women, on average, live several years longer because, unlike men, their hearts apparently suffer less age-related loss of strength over their lifetimes.

FACT: Women are not immortal, but in the UK for example, the number of female centenarians is still nine times more than men. On the other hand, the stress experienced by women trying to juggle a job with bringing up children is beginning seriously to affect their life expectancy in very significant ways. Additionally, recent American research showed that a mother, taking care, for example, of a chronically sick child, can add a decade or more to her biological age as a result of the prolonged stress involved.

FACT: On the health and smoking front, more and more European data indicates that lung cancer deaths are now one and a half times more likely in women than in men. That's an increase of a hundred and fifty percent over the last two decades compared with only a twenty percent increase for men.

FACT: Equally, alcohol abuse exacts a much greater physical toll on women, because they have a lower tolerance level. Since the early seventies, again in the UK, there has, consequently, been a seven-fold rise in deaths of thirty-five- to forty-four-year-old women from alcoholic cirrhosis. Figures are remarkably similar for most other western countries.

FACT: The male–female discrepancy is, according to various national and UN figures, in addition to the Y chromosome issue, also widely assumed to be due to macho male lifestyles: playing harder, working harder, doing more dangerous or manual tasks, and drinking and eating more than the female of the species. But see above and below for the interesting erosion of some of this differential.

FACT: Other good bits of internationally-relevant news for men is that they have most to gain from campaigns that advocate a better diet, less alcohol consumption, and better health and safety at work regulations. These are all beginning to reduce the comparative gender gap. Cut the booze, eat healthily, exercise, and that sexual bias is seen to narrow significantly.

FACT: But, and there's always a 'but' with statistics, biology and that Y chromosome still seem to wield a heavy ruler. For all the good news listed above, the longevity gap between genders may never be totally eliminated. Look, they say, at other mammals. Even outside nasty research laboratories where monkeys don't smoke, the females still outlive their partners. Even mummy whales outlive their mates by an average of thirty years.

And here's another 'but' to finish with. From all the above comes this exciting, though still much debated, statistic for men:

NEW FACT: It appears that if we strip out the numbers of men who, for all the above reasons, never reach their sixties, the Great Gender Divide reduces to a mere five years. We're working on it.

So is Darwin still at it? Is evolution to blame? Is the continuing male–female discrepancy largely to do with aggressive male competition and all that jazz? Partly, yes. It's still about the survival of the fittest and other latent aspects of natural selection. Males tend to compete more, and not just with fists, clubs, or weapons of mass destruction. Of course there are other contributory factors too. Young men up to, say, their mid-thirties, are greater risk-takers, and thus much more likely to die in road accidents or from drug abuse. Though hard evidence is difficult to come by and is often challenged by some experts, men in their youth in the majority of western countries are, according to some shocking statistics, also four times more likely to commit suicide than young women.

Otherwise, once they have made their sometimes very brief contribution to the breeding process, men are dispensable. Live fast, use testosterone in buckets, die young. So could castration, we wonder, be the answer to lengthier male lives? Since eunuchs are a dying breed, we might just get round to asking some medical biologist that question sometime, though it's difficult to be convinced that a pool of willing volunteers is out there, waiting to test that hypothesis.

THE FLIP SIDE

To generalize from all this, it's pretty clear that if boys were to eat their five portions of greens daily, cut out the heavy boozing, and run to the gym every day, they might catch up with girls in the course of time. On the other hand if we are hooked on cancer nails and smoke forty cigarettes a day (according to the *Lancet* – June 2005 – which reports a St Thomas's Hospital research report), our biological age will leap forward by seven and a half years, and if we are gluttons and obese, that jumps by an incredible nine years. So once more we see that mere chronological or numerical age is no guide to longevity.

A more drastic flip side to all this is the post- or Zip code lottery effect on health matters. This exists all over the western world. It is not necessarily just because of less effective medical services depending on where we live. Sadly, some areas, cities, even parts of cities, in all countries, have disastrously worse longevity (and infant mortality) statistics, due to local factors such as diet, climate, education, housing, ethnic diversity, and other issues of social deprivation. By contrast, some areas are statistically hugely healthier, so much so that they used to say that, in some such parts of rural Scotland they'd have to shoot someone to start a cemetery.

To give one extreme British example, life expectancy in post industrial Glasgow as a whole is eleven years less than for those living in East Dorset. But even within some towns such as Glasgow, a few blocks distance as to where one lives can make a huge difference to life expectancy. Another shocking example is within the English seaport of Bristol, where men in the Heartcliff area live on average *thirteen* years less than those living in upper-class Clifton (Sheffield and Bristol University Research, 2005).

All these huge social, hierarchical, and geographical differences depend on other fundamental factors such as our relative degree of affluence, our educational standards, as well as our current style of living. The above facts flag up the problems but don't necessarily suggest any easy solutions. They do however broaden our understanding of the issues involved. For instance, if in future far more people started living very much longer but in increasingly bad health, would that really make for a better society? Whatever else, put to one side those birthdays as measurements of age. Time on earth is elastic and depends heavily on all those physical and economic circumstances. It is a clear note of warning.

Statistics on ageing and the varied longevity of the sexes may appear a bit boring on the face of it, but they begin to underscore where we are now and what we should be doing about it. In this liberated, healthier, wealthier world of ours, a fifty-year-old can appear old, while someone of eighty-five can still be full of youth. We of *The Trailblazer Generation* need to realize from this that it can be a potential boom time for us all.

CHAPTER THREE

Cresting the Age Wave

"Tis easy to resign a toilsome place,
But not to manage leisure with a grace;
Absence of occupation is not rest,
A mind quite vacant is a mind distressed.'
— William Cowper

Cresting the Age Wave? Good concept maybe, but how do we get that wild wave to carry us forward on its crest and not sweep us under? We need to decide what we are looking for from now on. So far in life we've been shaped by how successful our careers have been; by good or bad fortune; by our genes; by chunks of happenstance. Now we have one more chance to start again and use our Freedom Years to great advantage. But as a first step, we have to get that pleasant or unpleasant step of our retirement out of the way. And that event can be more of a hurdle to surmount than we think.

This chapter examines and condemns many of the totally outdated retirement practices that are still endemic in most western countries. Before we do that however, let's establish some basic definitions. In the old days, most people assumed that work was work and play was play. But how exactly do people think of 'work' in these modern times? Earning money, gaining promotion in one form or another, enjoying the comradeship and excitement of business success, but probably also finding quite a lot of aggravation, boredom, and the constant repetition of unwanted tasks on the way. Increasingly over recent years, in many occupations, 'working hours' and holidays or Saturdays and Sundays of so-called 'leisure' have tended to blend too easily into one long continuum. That's because, particularly over the last few decades, if we are, or were, employed in professionally demanding jobs, we could

'Ah! The fertile lassitude of inactivity!'

– Victor Hugo

easily be tracked down electronically wherever we were, with new demands placed on us at any time of the day or night.

How do we define leisure? It usually conjures up images of doing something personally satisfying: vistas of long weekends, free time, quality time, down time, hobby time, days to pursue every personal passion, including, if we wish, total inactivity. But we all know that, in practice, there's little or no pleasure in having absolutely nothing to do. Leisure, say at those treasured weekends, consequently tends to get filled up with just as many niggling tasks as work. Domestic chores can be a real bore. Gardening, housework, repairs, shopping, looking after family members, even competing on the golf course or working out at the gym, can be both aggravating and unsettling. And in the background all the time is the excitement or bane of modern technology. Not just the telephone and TV, but e-mails, internetting, and all the rest, though if we handle things properly, the main technical component of control on all that remains us, ourselves.

As we approach or arrive at the day when post full-time employment begins, we rapidly need to repack-

age this whole work–leisure blend in our minds. The choice should largely be ours from now on. We ought to be able to lay all the old work stresses firmly aside. We should be able to add as much time off as we want to our new repertoire. We can decide to become armchair dynamos or we can go for long energetic walks without feeling guilty the whole time. No more clock-watching. No more struggling with those nasty tasks where our reach extended beyond our grasp. But we do still have to keep our senses in full working order by building up our resilience to the very different pressures of these new *Freedom Years*. Now, if we want real peace and quiet to contemplate the infinite, we should in principle be able to unplug the rest of the world. But no way should we decide to trade in work and the rush hours that went with it, for total idleness. There'll be plenty of time to sleep with the daisies later on.

The shock of adjusting from an eight-hour day on Friday, possibly via an emotional retirement party, to a totally empty Monday can be enormous. It can even feel a bit like having been given the sack. From that day on, it's so easy to become depressed, since we feel our skills are still in excellent working order and worthy of greater things. Some of us will rapidly and inevitably react by becoming despondent and lethargic. Turning in on ourselves is a frequent result of the sudden mental

starvation of all the group experiences and challenges we found in the workplace. We desperately need a bit of planning to avoid that big black hole.

QUEST FOR THE BEST

Yuk, you may say. This book's beginning to read like a motivational, self-improvement manual. Hold on! What's wrong with a handful of thought-provoking suggestions, even if we decide to ignore some of them? Haven't we all gone through life listening to the distilled ideas of others? Yes, of course as we grow older we don't want to be lectured to about when or where or what we should or should not be doing. Quite right, too. But since far too many of us on that critical cusp of retiring *make no preparations whatsoever*, what's on offer here are some crisp tactical ideas of take-it-or-leave-it advice and warning about growing old constructively and gracefully – or a fraction disgracefully if we prefer.

We don't need an exit ticket from the past, we need a first class ticket to the future. When we turn up at airports the check-in desk clerk always asks, 'Did you pack this suitcase yourself?' If for some reason we don't normally pack our own suitcases, on this particular journey we have to. The baggage we take with us from now on has to be personally selected by us alone. So don't start off by packing those mental carpet slippers, and banish the thought of bringing along some thread-bare easy chair that looks as if its sagging upholstery is ready and waiting to support our idleness. Unless we pack things that allow us to stay turned on and tuned in, we'll sit with boredom as a companion in front of the sinking fire of our lives.

When we take a flight, we often have to change planes at some terminal en route. Terminal's a pretty stupid term for an airport that's not our end destination. And it's not the best word to use in life either. It's like that bleak word retirement itself, which we'll come to realize is increasingly becoming an anachronism. It has a particularly debilitating resonance about it. In motoring terms a 'retread' has long been considered a derogatory term, but it's actually preferable when we reach this stage in life, since it can last longer than the original tyre. So let's retread ourselves, revitalize, reinvigorate, reinvent, recreate, revivify ... there are lots of 're-' words to choose from, and let's jettison this negative word retirement as soon as we can.

This is because there still is an all too prevalent belief hanging around that, in the words of the late Alistair Cooke, retirement is the first step to the grave. It's probably why he kept on working until he was ninety-five. Even government pensions agencies are working on the expectation that in three decades' time the average male life expectancy in the western world will be over ninety, so members of *The Trailblazer Generation* need to realize that, with all that extra time ahead, they have to work out a second life plan or career structure, with totally reformulated ambitions and goals. This probably will have to be achieved without the formalities of our previous employment, its office structures and the other back-up that we have long been used to. To quote a wonderful old Irish lady, we also need 'to gain a new conceit of ourselves', not only in our own eyes but also of those around us.

GET OUT AND GET ON

The Age Wave sweeps inevitably onwards. Despite the fact that we are living those longer, healthier, and more active lives, too many people are compulsorily retired at far too early an age. Many retired should not be retiring. Through long-established and increasingly questioned custom, this practice still happens without due attention being paid to the increasingly healthy ticking of our modern biological clocks. Retirement in the west still tends to take place in both the public and private sectors somewhere between the ages of sixty and sixty-five. But happily there is, throughout these developed economies, a growing campaign to do away with the whole concept of those mandatory cut-off dates. 'What will you do when you retire?' was an unknown question in the distant past when people never lived long enough to do so. It will become so once again, as most people become prepared actively to change gear. We need to start throwing away all the old maps and buying new ones which demystify old age and guide us to novel destinations. Instead retirement as a word might be redefined as *The Switchover*, the Turnaround Stage, the Third Wind, the Great Climacteric, the opportunity for a new energy to flow through our veins.

The British Department of Work and Pensions has already started climbing on the bandwagon by forecasting that set retirement ages will quite probably be swept away for ever as early as 2011. If and when that happens, it will allow us to appreciate even more than we do now that coming to the end of one long-term job is in no way a terminal, but merely a staging post in a far longer journey. If we think about it, it's totally nonsensical to go into an office and work flat out, a hundred percent of the time one day, and then be forced to switch down to zero the very next. That's why the current bureaucratic retirement culture needs to be replaced by programmes of phased retirement, job-sharing, or gradually working reduced hours. Some companies, like British Telecom, for example, are wisely introducing just such practices. Others, particularly the more intelligent banks in Europe and the United States, have deliberately begun to hire or rehire retired staff on a part-time basis, to deal with rich customers of their own age groups. Again, in the United States, NASA, as recently as 2002, reported that they had three times the number of employees over sixty than under thirty. That seems a good model to follow. By the way, it's fascinating to realize that while much of their research, particularly in the sciences, was carried out in their younger days, the vast majority of the recipients of Nobel Prizes in recent years have all been well over sixty. We can and should have confidence that this trend of recognizing the intellectual strengths of age will continue to grow.

A PLAN FOR ALL SEASONS

Given the choice, and given current governmental policies and guidelines in most of the developed economies, when and at what age should we ideally ease ourselves out of full time work? A diplomat is said to be someone who knows a woman's birthday, but not her age. We don't need to guess the age of older diplomats in Britain. Currently, even top ambassadors and other senior Foreign Office men and women are forced to retire precisely on their sixtieth birthday. There's absolutely no flexibility, though most of those diplomats are still at the very peak of their powers, experience, and abilities. Some of them, if they have served in tropical or other designated 'hardship posts', chalk up a number of extra pension-boosting years, and can retire at 'nominal sixty'. This can mean that they may only have reached the numerical age of fifty-seven, which is even more absurd. The result is that many of them go off with reasonable public service pensions in their pockets, and find exciting new careers in the City, or academia, or coining it in commerce. In the US State Department, by contrast, retirement comes at a more sensible sixty-six. Their Scandinavian counterparts have long had to serve on to the even more sensible age of sixty-seven, when these diplomats arrive at what the Norwegians call the 'dessert' or sweet course, generation. But why any of those outdated dates? Why not allow employees to remain on the books as long as they are willing or fully capable of carrying out their tasks?

Employers throughout the 'rich' world of course argue that keeping people on for too long prevents new blood flowing into the system. General de Gaulle famously wrote that the secret of success in government was not to let men grow old in their jobs. In addition many others argue that it's not worth the money training anyone over fifty to keep up to date. Now there's one thing we all can immediately and seriously disagree about. Let's take a moment to look at some other hard facts. As life expectancy is continuing to grow by about one year every four years in most of the developed world, things are going to get more and more difficult for those blinkered employers, and for governments, unless they wake up and do something about it. They need to *encourage* the continued employment of older age groups rather than putting them out to grass as they do now. Current, so-called 'best business practice' is also going to have to change. But hope is at hand. Governments are beginning to realise that in the high wind of reason such ridiculous old turkeys will get blown away for ever.

We are beginning to see other belated questionings of those mandatory retirement ages. Largely for financial and fiscal reasons, such practices will be forcibly consigned to what western governments are starting to call 'the dustbin of social history'. Wise commentators realize that both public and private sector employers will be forced to think anew, not just because they can't afford all the concomitant state and private pension payments, but for two other long-neglected reasons. First, it keeps us all working for longer so we keep paying income tax on full salaries to the state for many more years. Second, and more constructively, the hugely rewarding wisdom and experience of age can continue to be harnessed for decades longer than heretofore. As an extension to that, a recent survey found that in Britain, while around ten percent of pensioners who had reached the state retirement age were still working, nearly fifty percent of them wanted to work beyond that age, and around twenty-five per-cent said that they would keep on working until they were forced to stop. Good on them.

By contrast, British public sector labour unions constantly protest or threaten to strike over moving retirement dates from sixty up to sixty-five. Are they not desperately wrong? If they win, they'll bankrupt the Treasury. But why on earth do they continually cam-paign to put thousands of their own members onto the scrapheap when they still have so much going for them? Dead-hand bureaucracy of course saps so much initiative, and there are some diabolically boring jobs in the public sector, so it's easy to understand why some of those employees want to escape as soon as they can. But a majority in their late fifties or early sixties don't want to give up work when there are still so many things to do, if it's only minting more money to live on. If we work in the private sector we may feel a bit aggrieved by all this. We stay employed well into our mid sixties, paying our well-earned tax money into the state's coffers and thereby subsidizing the pensions of all those millions of public sector workers who are forced to retire at sixty. Is that fair?

There is also a battle with those private sector employers. They generally want the retirement age to remain at sixty-five, with the vague possibility of employees being allowed to 'request' to stay on. They do so, they argue, in order to create space for the young, and to get rid of those of us who are well past our sell-by date. But that latter problem can surely be better solved with the help of an annual medical and a job appraisal. In any case, with low birth rates and increasing barriers being introduced to skilled immigration, there isn't going to be much of a shortage of employment opportunities. With the exception of those who need their muscles and brains to defend us, such as members of the armed forces, the police, and, most certainly, judges, the battle cry must be *Ditch statutory retirement ages now!*

Statistics throughout the developed world demonstrate that professionals and other higher social groups survive on average five years longer than manual workers. Following from this one suggestion currently being explored in Britain is that people with university degrees might therefore be barred from receiving a state pension until they reach seventy, to reflect their longer life expectancies. Lower paid workers by contrast could then be able to draw theirs at sixty-five. In addition, in certain parts of any developed country, for example in the old industrial or mining areas, manual workers live out their retirement in poorer health. While there might be a bit of a good idea embedded somewhere in differentiating between types of retirees, the widespread reaction to this is that it would prove to be totally unworkable in practice. Western politicians need to become much more aware of the holes they are digging for themselves by not tackling these basic retirement issues. They try to rule our lives, but they will also retire. They'll leave office before the skies darken with their various foolish chickens coming home to roost. Hopefully more mature politicians, wielding greatly increased amounts of Grey Power, will change all that in the course of time. On which political subject, more later.

OLD BOLD OPTIONS

The wish fully to retire or not to retire at a certain point in life depends on what we've been doing up till now, and where we've been doing it. Take the teaching profession as an example. In our youth, particularly during or just after the Second World War, because younger men and women were serving in the armed forces, many of our best teachers were a long way past their traditional retirement date. From that experience we could argue many seventy or even eighty-year-olds would still make better teachers than some who are in their early twenties. If we were serving in that profession, we would be justified in campaigning to have the retirement age lifted a decade or removed altogether. In the countryside and in most rural communities there tend to be fewer problems over the age at which one retires. Those working in agriculture have always gone on for as long as they were physically able, with little thought of the idea of retirement. Farmers in most countries work till they themselves decide to stop, just as local village postmistresses used to serve their communities for as long as they too were healthy and mentally able to run the shop.

So what other retirement options are there out there? Answer: lots! What about choosing early retirement for example? Should this be encouraged or allowed without some strong financial disincentive? If for example we were to retire at fifty-five, that would mean that we had three or more decades of *not* contributing to the state's coffers ahead of us, except of course through paying the Exchequer for those parts of our pensions that are taxable. Even if we up-sticks and move abroad, would any state not be justified in coming running after us, to make us continue to pay our way?

Or what about adopting some of those partial retirement schemes? If we want to avoid a sudden change, and if we can arrange it, why not wind down gradually? Should modern employers not be encouraged or required to allow us to work for only part of the day, or for two or three days each week, rather than have us leave on the spot? That option would allow us to break ourselves more gently into our new lives. If we intend to make a complete break with the past and collect stamps or do the garden all day and every day for the rest of our lives, so be it. But we need to remember that, whether we work or play, the days still have the same number of hours in them. Pursuing hobbies and pastimes suit many of us, but there should be more ways available for easing ourselves slowly from full-time work into a new 'mixed' regime to give us time to adjust. It's a great option for us if we can arrange it, and it could also be valuable for employers as they bring new recruits in to learn from our experience.

Then there's the work-till-we-drop scenario. 'Work is much more fun than fun', claimed Noel Coward. 'The man who works, and is never bored, is never old', added the musician Pablo Casals. Millions of people in exciting, meaningful occupations will agree with them both. Continuing to keep on working for as long as possible is the ambition of many, particularly professional people. They say they will never ever retire.

> *'One's prime is elusive. You little girls, when you grow up, must be on the alert to recognise your prime at what ever time of your life it may occur. You must then live it to the full.'*
>
> *– Muriel Spark*

There are many arguments in favour of that course of action, but they need to keep an eye open for the burnout factor. It too can kill.

Ambition often drives people so hard that they work themselves to death in order to live better. There's more to life than being constantly 'busy', but any artist will continue to paint, any musician will continue to play, and a writer is seldom going to stop writing. We all know a number of skilled tradesmen who are equally determined to work as long as they are physically able, and teachers who will continue to give lessons, perhaps privately, as long as they are capable of doing so.

TROUBLE AND STRIFE

It's always dangerous for a male author to attempt to look at crucial matters such as retirement from a female perspective. This author does his best. That point made, it used to be said that the ten best years of a woman's life lay between thirty-nine and forty. Now, from a recent personal survey, these ten best years quite definitely lie between fifty-nine and sixty. With this in mind, any male author also has to avoid making any chauvinist judgements on such matters; no doubt there are those out there who will make it known if that fails to impress.

That said, it would be wrong *not* to consider the fact that a wife may well have been married to her partner for a good many years. For the first five or six of these, she may have pursued her own career. Then came children perhaps, and back in the sixties and seventies it was uncommon, even for career women, to go back to work while the offspring were still small, unless the family was very hard up. So, one way or another, for, say, the past thirty years, the husband, or partner, went off to the office at 7.30 in the morning, and came back twelve hours later. Now comes his retirement from full-time work. And he thinks it's just *his* life that's about to change. What about his wife and her career? He maybe wants to be up at all odd hours, have that leisurely breakfast, then hang around getting in her way, reading his paper till half way through the morning, making constant cups of coffee, interrupting her and totally upsetting her previous lifestyle. What about her own working life, her domestic duties, her social life, and, above all, her body space? She's got much more to do than making jam and baking cakes for the next Women's Institute fête.

What does bridge the gender gap at this stage in life, is that relationships come into their own once more. Male or female, we have totally forgotten what it's like living with some-one twenty-four hours a day, seven days a week. Remember all the little stresses and strains when we first got married or started living together? The dirty socks steeping in the hand-basin?

'Will you still need me, will you still feed me, when I'm sixty-four?'
– Lennon and McCartney

HIS AFTERNOONS ARE
GIVEN OVER TO 'POWER
NAPPING' AS HE CALLS
IT...

The nasty practice of washing the dishes before rather than after a meal, and a host of other little idiosyncrasies? Now we have to learn how to cope all over again, full-time and several decades later.

Retirement can mean half the money and twice the time with one's spouse. As we've seen, most men reaching retirement don't even begin to appreciate how much of a shock this will come to their wives' peace and tranquillity. A true story here: a friend admitted that she used to say how much she was looking forward to her husband's retirement, and that she couldn't wait to share long leisurely lunches with him. Some hope! On day three of his retirement, she admitted to hearing herself yelling at him, 'You're not going to be hanging around waiting for me to cook you lunch every day, are you?' No, we may have married for richer or for poorer, but certainly not for lunch together every day.

'My wife and I tried two or three times in the last forty years to have breakfast together, but it was so disagreeable we had to stop.'
– Winston Churchill

These are not uncommon issues, and though they are sometimes quite difficult to confront, we all know couples who live reasonably happily together but, for body space reasons, routinely dine separately to give each other their space. It's like that old Jack Benny story about finding happiness in marriage. 'My wife and I never forget the importance of our nights out: a nice cosy little restaurant, soft lights, good wine, music, and dancing … She goes on Tuesdays … I go on Thursdays.'

But there are many good sides too. After both partners have retired they have a great opportunity to get to know each other once more, and togetherness can end up being no bad thing. Wives can relearn how to get their husbands to be useful around the house, particularly if they hint that they think they're getting

too old to do anything worthwhile. We're also going to have to plan jointly about how to manage our money in future, which may push us both into looking at common options that save some expense or produce a little extra cash on the side. More on that later.

Given the tendency for men to marry women younger than themselves, and the longevity gap that still exists between the sexes, widowhood is a commoner outcome than widower-hood. Subsequent loneliness can become a problem. We're never alone with a clone, but if we suddenly have to live on our own because death takes our partner from us, it can be highly traumatic. Adjusting can be tricky, but flying solo can, with determination, turn out to be pleasurable in the long run. It's a brave new world out there. We mustn't hide or stay locked in. We may need help to step out of our box. But being single again can actually turn out to be productive, particularly if our mate, of whatever sex, tended to be dominant in our relationship.

In the old days, people seldom moved from the professional area or working environment into which they stepped at the beginning of their adult lives. All that is changing. With more flexible work patterns, retirement is absolutely not the end of the line any more. It should be an outmoded concept in mandatory terms, but as long as it still exists, it has to be seen as an open gate to the future. We should be looking at a range of strategies, such as phased or partial retirement, or working as long as we wish or are capable. Now we have the opportunity of moving into totally new fields at a pace to suit ourselves, developing new skills and using old ones. We and our partners need to go with the flow as we ride the age wave into the future.

CHAPTER FOUR

Switchover Tactics

'Fear not for the future, weep not for the past.'
– Percy Bysshe Shelley

A ge is the high price we all pay for becoming mature. Our talents have no age however, so now's the time to challenge ourselves by thinking seriously about how to use them in the future. Why? Because international statistics show conclusively that a sure and certain way of curtailing our lives, even though we may have an overwhelming ambition to lead a quieter life from now on, is to lapse into total inactivity after full-time work. That certain fact should spur us to start planning how we're going to make that great leap forward well in advance of our due retirement date. Or, if we're there already, we should start today. Which is what this chapter is all about.

A lot of people tend to shy away from any such decisions. Why bother? We find lots of excuses. We're going to need time to break out of all our old life patterns. With so much leisure time coming up, we can take as long as we want to readjust. Others permanently detach themselves from taking any positive action at all, and that helps scupper their future. There's a totally new season ahead of us, and we really have to kit ourselves out to handle it properly. OK, seasons in nature don't advance: they are cyclical and repeat themselves. It's all a bit like gardening: plants need re-potting from time to time, and that time is now.

Other equally negative arguments are invented. We can only sit on one chair at a time, only eat one meal, sleep in one bed, only read one book. We've probably accumulated as many goodies as we need over the years: house, fridge, cooker, TV, laptop. Except for the very poorest, we're all more or less the same in this regard. Enough possessions are enough. We've worked hard, done our bit, and that's sufficient. As we're not going to starve, why should we worry about the future? We want to relax and enjoy life. We have sufficient comfort, money, happiness. It may be a supercharged cliché, this concept of 'cup full', but it's a pertinent one. Why strive for anything more? The answer to all that again is that we've got to watch that we don't drift into becoming satiated Mogadon beings, perpetually couch-potato-ing in front of daytime TV.

If we accept this warning, let's have a look at what our switchover tactics might be. How can we create an active retirement strategy? We don't quite know what exactly is going to hit us, so there's a real need to point out some of the many opportunities and unexpected pitfalls with which we may be faced. We're no longer playing the old familiar career survival game. *Let's live till we die!* is the new slogan. *Die alive!* is another way of putting it. As one British businessman used to say, 'I'll never retire. I'll still be arguing to get a better deal when they nail me into my coffin.'

THE TRAILBLAZER GENERATION'S NINE POINT PLAN

From surveys of the views of groups of members of *The Trailblazer Generation*, here are some key issues to consider. We need to …

1 Recognize, though it may be difficult, that we can't just stand still with so many years ahead of us.

2 Accept that we are going to have to re-brand ourselves, and work out how to strike that balance between a creative future and leisure time.

3 Compile a stock-check of our present position and commitments: the ongoing skills we're taking with us, our family circumstances, pensions, other money matters, and so on.

4 Work through a whole range of out-of-our-previous-box options. What do we want to achieve that we haven't achieved so far in life?

5 List our options and strategies for doing so.

6 Set out an agenda for change, and decide where and how we're going to erect our new stall.

7 List the likely barriers and problems we envisage meeting on the way.

8 Target the door-opening opportunities and old contacts we think may help us.

9 Start with Point One above.

Looking at that list immediately drags a lot of problems to the surface. For a start, *Point One* above may seem a bit banal, but we've all felt, at one time or another, quite surprised by what age we've actually reached, and realized that we've still got all those years ahead of us. But how on earth do we action *Point Two*, and start re-branding ourselves at this late stage in our lives? No problem: once we've decided on our agenda, we've got to make it clear to anyone who matters what we intend to do in future. But there are bits of downside to ditch on the way.

Planning ahead can initially make us feel a bit inadequate. This is largely because we've been programmed to believe that retirees aren't capable of making much of a contribution from now on. We may also have inherited the credo that at the very top of the Sin List is idleness. Now that we've left our desks or conveyer belts, we're going to turn into good for nothing wastrels, with the devil lurking around maliciously looking for work for our idle hands. *Get thee behind me, Satan* is the battle cry on that score. But if we spend too much time killing time it will kill us. Unstructured living really is an unseen danger. Any psychologist will warn us that it can be both unsettling and dispiriting. It's akin to the old saying that a perpetual holiday is an apt description of hell, though if we look back at such so-called holidays in the past, we probably recall that we often seemed to work twice as hard during them as we did when we were meant to be working.

We're not becoming spongers. We're going to continue to contribute to the good of ourselves, our families, and society, just as we did in the past. We must never think of ourselves as unemployed, since that has an unnecessarily negative ring to it. Nor have we become passengers or drones. Yes, it's easy to get depressed by suddenly not having a workplace to travel to each day. But instead we're about to discover what's called *creative leisure.*

STOCK-CHECKING

Now we need to act on *Point Three* above and tally up our resources to avoid such a progression of empty days. There's no need to rush things too much. Few issues are important, and of these even fewer are very important. We can simplify our new ambitions, and how we are going to go about achieving them. Then, if it doesn't sound like banal sermonizing, let's leave the pains and passions of the past behind us, and start climbing that totally new flight of stairs.

What form should a personal stock-check take? First of all, what's in our war chest? We know our various talents but how often were they camouflaged or misused in the past by the work we were obliged to carry out? What skills haven't we been using up till now? Here's a starter pack of issues, some of which were again polled from groups of *The Trailblazer Generation.* Do we have …

---

1 Enough money to do what we really want to do?
2 Sufficiently good personal insurance policies to underwrite the above if anything goes wrong?
3 A happy and safe home?
4 Reasonably good health?
5 Friends and relations who will support us in what we intend to do? (Though always remember that they're numerically ageing at the same rate as us.)
6 A backup of familiar values by which we are used to being surrounded?
7 An otherwise stable lifestyle?

> 8 A clear idea of the issues we're going to have to face? Some may be a bit unexpected, surprising, or even dangerous.

THE JOYS OF LAZINESS?

It is so easy to throw all such lists aside. Why on earth bother with them? Because all progress through life is by a winding stair, and we've got to work out which is the right one to take. The old proverb says that an idle brain is the devil's workshop. Or listen to Leonardo da Vinci's belief that *Inaction saps the vigours of the mind.* Or Arnold Bennett's underlining of modern medicine's belief that *Inactive people age twice as fast.* Laziness can grow like a bad habit. Its cobwebs can quickly tie us up tight. If we believe we've accomplished everything we want to accomplish, then we're ready for the grave.

Permanent inaction is pure misery. We all know people who suffer badly from this complaint. So let's consider how those psychologists suggest countering the highly dangerous ploy of lapsing into mindless passivity. Some propose confronting it by getting us to 'find our flow', in other words identifying with some project or activity that grips our full attention and matches our capabilities. Not a bad idea finding whatever resonates with the mature us. So let's marshal our untapped skills and tap them. That's one key to re-branding ourselves.

We've all acquired habits that can mar or shorten our lives. Yes, there are bound to be other downside factors in our way. We were disciplined by our work. Once that disappears, which can happen after a very short period of time, we now need some personal rules to abide by. We can easily feel more than a bit lost without them. Our suddenly un-busy life can also lead to ordinary, day-to-day tasks seeming much more difficult to handle. As a result, other fundamental questions confront us.

- What on earth are the coming decades really going to offer us?
- What are our best hopes and worst fears for those decades?
- How much new life will we really manage to squeeze out of them?
- We used to be steered through our careers by our employers. Who's going to help and advise us now?

We need to summon up quite a few ergs of extra energy at this key moment in our lifecycle. It's our decision time now. Grab those new opportunities. Forgive the repetition of that Latin tag, *Carpe Diem*! Don't delay. Procrastination kills. This is our *O B C*

– our *One Big Chance* to do something totally different from now on.

NOTHING VENTURED

Rupert Murdoch, a man rarely starved of an opinion, once remarked that he disliked his editors changing the format of his newspapers, like moving sport from the back pages to the middle and so on. 'My readers', he went on, 'like to know where their marmalade is each morning.' Good point. Certain schedules and routines need to be thought out and practised at this critically challenging point in life. Without disciplining ourselves with some established practices such as we've had to adhere to in our past work schedules, we can so easily slip into the black pit of lethargy. We've seen it happen to others, drifting from sleep to food, to nap to food, to nap to drink, to food to bed. 'We have to get up early if we want to get out of bed,' Groucho Marx remarked. He was so right.

From a recent survey of around fifty people who were about to join, or had just joined, *The Trailblazer Generation*, here's yet another list of self-disciplinary rules drawn from some of their own experiences.

1   Get up reasonably early.
2   Try to keep to a brisk, start-the-day schedule.
3   Exercise in some way every day.

4   Have something to do or look forward to each morning.
5   But don't let it become obsessive.
6   Keep trying out something new.
7   Keep a diary and a list of key projects to think about.

Such minor prompts may seem simplistic, but all these people spoke from experience and agreed that if we don't establish routines of one sort or another, it can lead to disaster. All boats of our age rise and fall with the same time and tide, so, staying with the nautical illustration, we've got to decide whether to remain anchored and let the barnacles grow around us, or slip moorings and set sail towards new horizons. OK, it's an over-ripe metaphor perhaps, but metaphors are always handy in showing up the truth.

DISCIPLINE, DISCIPLINE, DISCIPLINE

'A foolish consistency is the Hobgoblin of little minds.'
– Ralph Waldo Emerson

You're right, Waldo, but a bit of that self-discipline really is critical. Now that we have a seven day weekend to play with, it doesn't stop us totally rescheduling our lives. Our weekly and monthly planning charts can be as highly elastic as we want them to be. Want to pay all the bills and answer

all the e-mails late on a Sunday evening? Why not? Get up when we feel like it, and go to the cinema or the gym on a Monday morning or a Tuesday afternoon? Go for it. Shop at a quiet time on a Wednesday? Do it. Take time out and wander across the hills thinking thoughts inspiring or poetical? Now it's all ours to choose.

We don't need to keep pulling ourselves up by the roots to see how we're getting on, but we should always keep a bit of a check on our progress. We've got lots of time to soar above the routine dross of the past and experience life's exhilarating highs. 'The fundamental things apply, as time goes by' were the words of the famous song. Unplug the television, listen to great music, read all the books we've never read. Or keep the telly and overuse the DVD player by settling back and watching all the stacks of great movies we've missed over the years. We have time to cater to all our preferences. Can't stand reality TV? Just like watching news and documentaries? Like old style dancing, and amusing rather than horror films at the cinema? No worries, as the Australians say. We need to follow where our mood takes us from now on. Banish stress. Feel no guilt. And make good use of that mental 'off' button to kill any disagreeable parts of life.

Having some structure like this is great. We can add that from now on we don't need to do a lot of things we've never liked doing. We can avoid people who don't suit us. We don't have to work with or relate to them any more. We would all still quite like to meet one or two famous individuals, but there are some we hope we'll never meet again, even to the extent of not much minding reading their obituaries before our own death notice appears in print. If we're travelling, there's no need to yell at the girl behind the check-in desk because the plane's running late. There are no meetings we're running late for. Put the feet up instead. Our life is ours. Yes, be punctual, if that's part of our mind-set, and it's only polite after all. But above all, bin all those stresses and strains which came from goals missed, strategies delivered late, tasks being left undone. There's a lot that's splendid about the *mañana* approach to life. But, deep down, still keep a very firm grip on what today is all about.

We may be living through *The Freedom Years*, but having absolutely nothing constructive to do can actually turn out to be pretty stressful. It doesn't always make us feel carefree. It may sound odd, but we really can suffer from an absence of problems. There still are decisions we can take and choices we can make, though we probably found some of them easier to grapple with when we lived and worked in a more structured environment. If we get into the habit of wakening early,

and as we grow older such things tend to happen, we don't need to lie there until some standard getting-out-of-bed time. Get up when we feel like it. Do some early morning chores: letters, bill-paying, polishing the silver, with no one (having appeased the spouse of course, otherwise it could lead to marital meltdown) to disturb us, and no phones ringing. Then, when the morning comes along, have a nice leisurely breakfast with all that behind us. Enjoy quality time with those with whom we live and love. Go back to bed? Why not? Churchill did so after breakfast, and he still ran a country and won a war. Redistribute hours to suit our needs.

Happiness can't buy us money. Happiness can mean a bad memory. Some people bring happiness with them when they arrive, others when they leave us. Mrs Thatcher said that happiness was a ticked off list. No need to do it her way either, but all those lists can be useful in building structure into our new lives. Think of all the concurrent joys! No using up bags of frustrated anger sitting in traffic jams or on delayed and crowded commuter trains. Have a long bath instead. Read the paper from cover to cover. It was once called *flexitime*: this symbiosis between tasks and play. The day is ours.

Technology creeps in here. In the good old days we used to sit around waiting for the postman. Now we get a reply seconds after our e-mail message is sent, and not several first-class-post-days later. We can reply or ignore messages as we choose. Technology frees up lots of time to do other things, though there's always a lurking temptation to fill up that extra time with more and more e-mailing. Technology cuts both ways. It's exciting, amazing, innovative, enabling and always breaking new barriers. The danger is that, once we get hooked, and there are many organizations these days specially equipped to train people of *The Trailblazer Generation*, we are just as likely to spend long hours enslaved to the Internet, for good or naughty reasons, as any teenager.

Reputations are not built on what we intend to do. We maybe also need this self-discipline to stop ourselves slouching around from daybreak till bedtime. All this free time can become a *Big Domestic Issue* as well. Maybe our partner makes it impossible to act as freely as we might wish, because we're upsetting their routines, their housework, their body space. Divorce can become an option if we do actually spring out of bed at four each morning and spend the next hour or three crashing around waking everyone else up in the process. Nonetheless, new habits, backed up by a bit of living on autopilot, are worth thinking about.

Back to basics once more. What's meant by a good lifestyle? It's highly subjective. To some it's staying in bed all day and partying all night. To others it's about being as active as we have ever been. Here's another list of positives, some of them drawn from the same groups of *The Trailblazer Generation*, for us to doodle with:

1 Keep taking decisions. Don't let things drift.
2 Maintain the life we want to live for as long as possible, and our freedom to choose.
3 Do not give up our independence before we have to.
4 Safeguard our ability to take any important decisions that might affect us in the future.
5 Keep up that pattern of healthy activity. No need to climb mountains if we don't like heights.
6 Build a routine that encourages or protects our self-esteem.
7 Do something constructive each day. It makes us feel fulfilled if we earn an occasional pat on the back from those around us.
8 Reward ourselves with what we like doing most. Protect our feelings of self-worth.

Yet more lists! Who needs them? We only get this old once. Forget all that self-discipline nonsense and just enjoy. There's always going to be something out there to look forward to, be it a bit of travel, a visit to a museum, a trip to the theatre. Why plan for anything more? Because half a plan, like a half brick, can do a lot of damage. We had to programme ahead during our working lives. But as we've seen, many people seem to stop doing that from the very moment they retire. They become complacent or they drift. If we're of a mind to prevent this happening to us, we need to think hard about most of these issues.

Here's one typical example, taken from an earlier age group, of this sort of dangerously negative mind-set. Head-hunters often find when they suggest to adults in their late forties and early fifties who are stuck in some boring mid-life job, that they might consider undertaking a career change. A huge number of them tend to reply that they're already well past that sort of thing.

'I'm far too old,' they say. 'I'm already forty, forty-five, fifty,' they add.

To which many a head-hunter's response will be, 'Great! That means you still have several lively decades ahead of you.'

'But we can't change; we can't have it all any more,' they go on to moan. They say they want continuity of work, family, friends, sports, and lots of money … Change would upset it all. They probably never did have all this in the first place.

People can or should be marketable at almost any age, provided they are healthy enough and have kept up to date with their skills. The key message here is that it's our perceptions of ourselves that need to alter. Whatever our age, we have to remove the stabilizers and go with the roll. But going forward by picking the low-hanging fruit is often too easy an option. Proper adjustment to *The Freedom Years* needs some tough new house training.

A close friend retired recently from forty years of public service. He had, throughout that time, always been surrounded by diary secretaries, research assistants, and a chauffeur to see him through his workload. Yes, that friend did have a desk at home, in his so-called study, but that was largely to deal with the clutter of domestic matters which he shared with his wife. Visiting him there, he was seen trying to deal with his morning mail. We suddenly realized that he had hardly opened an envelope in years, much less knew how much a first class stamp cost, or how to find a telephone number. He had even been dictating e-mails to his delectable secretary till the very evening that he finally left his office. It recalls Sir Malcolm Rifkind's story of being asked by a journalist what it was like no longer being British Foreign Secretary, shortly after he was defeated in the 1998 General Election. 'Oh it's not that different,' he replied casually. 'I get up in the morning, wash and shave, have breakfast with my wife, pick up my briefcase, then go outside and jump into the back of the car … And find it doesn't go anywhere.'

Another friend, having spent a lifetime running a family business from scratch, and building it up into something quite prosperous, found, from one day to the next, sudden retirement desperately shocking. He had reached his apotheosis too soon, of his own volition, by deciding to quit and leave the running of the company to his sons. He'd planned it carefully, the handover of the business, that is. He was equally determined that, when he left, he was not going to hang around, and that was that. What he had *not* planned with sufficient care was what *he* was going to do next. That revelation hit him with a thud, and a period of serious depression followed, not least because it also affected his wife and her domestic lifestyle. The good news is that he got over it pretty quickly, creating a new and active life for himself. But he admits he was wrong not to prepare himself. So let's do just that.

OPPORTUNITY KNOCKS

We've no excuses any longer, remember. We've entered *The Freedom Years*, and they really are as free as we want to make them. We can set our own goals. We need to watch that a 'don't have time' attitude doesn't change into 'can't be bothered'. It's an easy slip.

Let's list some exciting opportunities we can all consider.

Further education. Why not think seriously about going back to university or college? Or, if we didn't first time round, going off to learn an entirely new academic discipline? No matter where we live, there are usually options for local training, or on residential courses, or by long-distance learning, as with Britain's Open University. We can also probably find organizations that help with the fees.

Voluntary work. Working for the good of the community – pro bono activity – can be hugely rewarding in a personal if not in any serious financial sense. There are masses of organizations out there in every rich country, and many poor ones too, desperately looking for the skills and experience many of us have. They won't be able to pay us much, except, perhaps, some modest expenses. There's a huge amount of satisfaction to be gained from giving time to a charity or some quasi-governmental organization, at home or overseas. From fundraising, to party political work, on which more anon, to getting into local community activities which we hadn't time to get involved with before, the range is enormous. Many organizations offer in-depth training to older volunteers for a range of their programmes, including working with young people, or in helping various other age groups with a range of management and technological skills.

Setting up a new business. This can be fun, challenging, and it may even make a bit of money on the side. Retirees we have interviewed run everything from minicab firms, to window cleaning, to headhunting-research consultancies. One retired architect in his sixties is now making a pile of money as an electrician, when he had hardly ever changed a light bulb in the past.

Part time work. The prospects and opportunities for *The Trailblazer Generation* are growing all the time. Some of the big supermarkets and do-it-yourself shops are getting increasingly happy to recruit the over-sixties, people with the time and patience to help customers, and who know from experience what they are talking about.

Consultancy work. Portfolio-living is a common step onwards from full-time work. We can build up a range of paid and unpaid activities, depending on how much we want to earn, and what amount of time we want to fill.

Writing. One increasingly common idea is to begin writing one's life history, or memoirs, or researching the family tree, not necessarily for publication, but for our family and friends. There are many people and their loved ones who have benefited enormously from this diversion.

Other activities. Now is the opportunity to expand, with a gigantic leap, and develop those hobby or leisure activities we've never had enough time to pursue. White water rafting? Why not? Learning to play a musical instrument, to sing, to paint or sculpt, or better our interest in anything from photography to ornithology. As a gateway to the future, there are many clubs and associations out there waiting for us to join them.

BACK TO SCHOOL

Of all the above, life-long education is the most popular, so let's look at it in a little more detail. Recent statistics on both sides of the Atlantic show remarkable numbers of even the over-seventies turning to further training. At the end of the dark and tedious tunnel, bleak with the drudgery of past employment, lots of educational excitements beckon. They can be academic or finding and developing new skills we didn't know we had in us. They can be taking up some vocational subject or practical trade.

'No wise man ever wished to be younger,' wrote Jonathan Swift, but lots of older people find a new life, surrounded by hordes of bright young students, remarkably stimulating. Adult education courses are packed with mature age groups, not least because many of them can benefit from reduced fees or from grants. One special example for the more mature is an academic campus outside Boston in the United States. It is one of dozens of university-linked retirement communities spread across that country. People well into their nineties, but with an average age of eighty-three, study law, music and the arts there. Other centres now exist to cater for would-be or professional academics who want to stay in touch with university life. Older generations often help young students on an unpaid basis at these highly vigorous campuses. There are dozens of opportunities for continuous learning, with participation at lectures and tutorials on an almost full-time basis.

Ageing students don't have to study any more but they do it for the joy of keeping on learning, and enjoying the delights of being a freshman all over again. In

Britain and Europe there are still far fewer opportunities such as these, but things are beginning to change under the aegis of the University of the Third Age. Many other agencies, both public and private, exist to help people of *The Trailblazer Generation* to find these educational openings. We can all help ourselves in this regard by recreating in part what we had before. Setting aside a room as a study, separate from our home if possible, is of huge assistance to both work and further study. Installing a different telephone line, laptop, desk, and efficient filing system, allows both us and our families to keep the space we enjoyed before. If we

play it right, life-long adult education only ends with death.

DO BEFORE WE DIE

The world is full of lots of other lists these days: things we cannot do without, things to do before we're fifty or sixty, and things to do before we die. It would be far better to call them a roll-call of future ambitions. We've all had them tucked at the back of our minds for most of our lives. There's bound to be some vital experience we still want to have, or a place we wish to visit, or a person we hope to meet before we pass on. On the other hand, as we age, many things we wanted to do when we were young, we no longer desire. There are few to-die-for branded goods on our shopping lists now, and our ambitions reduce considerably over the years. This author wrote once that, as he had seen Diana, Princess of Wales, dance with John Travolta at the White House, he was never again going to be fascinated by people dancing. Never wanted to climb Everest, parachute from an aircraft, nor hang-glide or bungee jump anywhere? There are lots of world destinations we have absolutely no wish to end up in, but a choice few things we still may wish to appreciate before the end. They are out there waiting for us.

This is it: our one and only chance. We of *The Trailblazer Generation* are where we are now. We need to stock-take, make a careful plan and then decide what our priorities are. How do we want to be branded: slippers, cardigans, and sitting around all day; or as real get-up-and-goers? We still have a huge contribution to make. Break out the new agendas and plan those Freedom Years to the full.

CHAPTER FIVE

Death to Ageism

'Youth would be an ideal state if it came a little later in life.'

– Herbert Asquith

As part of the process of maintaining and building on our aspirations for later life we have to contend not only with our own fallibilities, but also with ageism. Which is what this chapter intends to confront in all its forms. It exists to a greater or lesser degree within our immediate families, among our friends and associates, but also, and most importantly, in the institutional ageism that is still so prevalent throughout society generally. We find it embedded in governmental attitudes, among employers in both the public and the private sectors, among professionals, and even with some medical staff who should know better. Above all it lurks within the media which sets much of the agenda for public opinion.

THE FACT THAT WE ARE DISCUSSING SEPARATE BEDS AT ALL IMPLIES AN UNSPOKEN AGEISM IN OUR RELATIONSHIP.

Stereotypical ageist images are also commonplace in films, television and advertising. Dismissive words like grouchy, gaga, geriatric, or senile, are used indiscriminately, stigmatizing people who are still full of intellectual and physical life. With acerbic humour, our own generation can wryly refer to our 'twilight years' or 'eventide homes', but when younger age groups start patronising us, many retirees polled on this are ready to use their Zimmer frames as battering rams, or trade in their walking sticks for AK 47s. Here are some of their current pet hate words and expressions:

Blue Rinse Brigade; *Golden Oldies*; *Old Fogies*; *Dodderies*; *Grave-dodgers*; *Sun-setters*; *Wrinklies*; *Crumblies*; *Tail-end Lifers*; *Bus Passers*. Then there's *Twilight years*; *Gaga*; *Long in the tooth*; *Senior moments,* and on and on and on.

We win the occasional battle in the long war against ageism. A very rich old man lived in Chelsea, London, where it's always difficult to find a place to park. He drove a large, old-fashioned Rolls Royce, which he kept in pristine condition. One late afternoon, coming back from a day in the country, he had to drive around for quite a long time before he found a parking space big enough to fit. It was right next to a steel rubbish skip. As he started backing into the space, to his cold fury, a brash young man in a flash but tinny sports car drove in forwards, and usurped the space. The old man paused and wound down the window. The young man jumped out of his car, locked it, and, as he walked past, grinned, with the words, 'You have to be very young and very fit to do that, Granddad.' But he paused in his tracks, horrified, when the old man simply slipped his Rolls into reverse and continued to back into the space, squashing the sports car into a mashed-up heap against the immovable skip. When the furious young man came running up to him, the Rolls Royce driver smiled icily at him, and said, 'And you've got to be very old and very rich, to be able to do that, laddie.' Thankfully, there were lots of amused spectators there to defend him until the police arrived.

But we of *The Trailblazer Generation* have to be very careful when we attack ageism either in words or by our actions. If we do, we stand accused of being age-rage grumps or Saga louts, constantly moaning at the world around us. It is a fine line to tread. Expressions of outrage or frequent complaints, as we will discuss in a later chapter, are not the way to fight back. We have to attack it at its core. As in a swimming pool, most of the noise comes from youth at the shallow end. That's a bleak fact of life. But this strident tendency to stigmatise those who have retired or who are old, which sometimes is almost as bad as racism, doesn't just come from the young. It's rampant throughout the western world. Some of it is understandable. Youth, not unnaturally, looks at some aspects of the ageing process as akin to an illness. But ageism goes far further than that. Governments and public institutions are rife with the attitude that anyone over a certain age is past it. They may think us heroically splendid for having survived so long, but we're widely seen as increasingly decrepit and probably grumpy to boot.

It was not, and is not universally so. In other cultures, particularly in historical times – think of Greece and Rome – age was widely venerated. The old continued to rule, as they still partially do in China and in certain sections of society in the United States. But throughout most of the western world, and sadly in much of Asia, if we're over whatever the numerical figure is which defines the age when people retire, with the backing of the youth-obsessed media, we are perceived as being well on our way to the scrap-yard. Later on, when we move into our seventies or eighties, we're categorised as 'not quite dead yet.' If we fight against ageism, we tend to be branded as silly old pensioners or written off as professional moaners. These attitudes have to be confronted and condemned. In the process we need to avoid engaging in an all out age war, a subject often written about in the media. Youth is not our enemy. The path to defeating ageism is, however, through education and by example.

Because of these deep-seated institutionalized attitudes, individual members of *The Trailblazer Generation* have to look in more detail at how we win more positive recognition. The fight has to be a political one against the thoughtless, collective discrimination that exists throughout most of western society. It's a culture that has been embedded for too long in both behaviour and practice. The new middle-aged have to demonstrate by our actions that we are as lively and productive as we ever were. We have to ensure that the media reports our activities fairly and effectively.

Our latent political power is huge. Given that in Britain, for example, there are currently more members of the Royal Society for the Protection of Birds than there are in all the main political parties put together, it should not be too difficult for us to build up stronger Grey Power movements in the United Kingdom and elsewhere, using our financial strengths to get our opinions heard much more clearly. Little old ladies with handbags keeping their places in supermarket queues, indicate what power the old could wield if only we were better organized. But at a higher level we need to find ways of remaining longer and longer at the top of the dunghill of public and private life. And the key way of doing that is by using the media to show that our experience and talents are still crucial to society as a whole.

As we've seen from the statistics, the size and strength of the ageing populations of the western world have changed dramatically over recent decades. But there's little point in going round proclaiming that success if the rest of society simply fails to notice. Which is why those of *The Trailblazer Generation* with experience of public life have to try to remain centre stage, working longer but not growing old. And we need to be seen to be doing so. With most reasonable people we should have little difficulty in achieving these aims. Yet there's still that disparagingly offhand rather than deliberate tendency among some sections of society to belittle us, largely because of the traditional barriers of misunderstanding that have always existed between the ages. Thinking back in time we'll clearly remember this ourselves; we too had a variety of attitudes to the old, usually because of our own individual domestic experiences. Older people in some societies may once have been venerated, but now many of them provoke only pity, rejection or avoidance. Thoughtless remarks pop up all over the place. We've all heard them and maybe have used them ourselves. 'Poor old boy. He's losing his marbles.' 'A geriatric OAP', or 'She's years the wrong side of sixty …' are phrases heard on just one radio programme while this paragraph was being written. Also included were a host of patronizing if well-meant remarks like 'Isn't he remarkable for his age?'

Conventional attitudes like this are difficult to defeat. The contemporary media on both sides of the Atlantic and throughout most of the English-speaking world, is totally overwhelmed by youth culture. Given such a dominant climate, it's easy to see why age and experience are dramatically discounted. Yet we of the Third Age, as Americans call us (i.e. they've rolled Shakespeare's last two categories into one), are as much to blame as any other group. We've consistently failed to draw sufficient attention to the huge reserves of unused talent that are being binned by automatic retirement processes. To take one example: despite the huge size of the over sixties TV audiences, a recent American study showed that only three percent of characters appearing on television were over sixty-five. In Britain we can even find evidence, implausibly, that young actors are 'greyed-up' to look old in order to play senior citizens in dramas and advertisements. That's only a shade better than Johnny Carson's remark about a new invention for people who want to look young ... snap-on acne.

A gentle trawl through a single week's newspapers and magazines further reveals this tendency to belittle or mock age. At its core it's probably not meant to be unpleasant or malign, but it emerges that way.

Journalists casually or condescendingly refer to us as wrinkly old prunes when we've merely been matured by the sun of life. That's one reason why many older folk pull out of politics in later life: they can no longer stand the constant media attacks. But retaliating has to be planned with care. Those journalists have their articles to write against set deadlines. Sadly, the same subjects crop up again and again. Culled from that week's press coverage, comments were to be found on such subjects as the tired depth of the furrows around the eyes of the elderly, their flawed complexions, their hair loss, their tooth-decay, their hearing aids, their Zimmers, their stair and bath lifts. There's no point in getting angry at all this. We have to fight back in a clear and reasoned manner.

Age discrimination is not all to do with the media by any means. It is endemic in the public services. As a further example, look at one offshoot of the financial services sector: life insurance. The elderly, who need it most, often can't get cover, except, perhaps, for fire and theft. Or examine the conditions set by travel insurance companies which inflate premiums by up to a hundred percent or more for the over sixty-fives, imposing various additional tough restrictions, or frequently refusing to grant any cover whatsoever. With around ten million people over sixty-five in Britain, sometime soon, given the gigantic grey pound spend on travel, the insurance business is going to have to come off its ageist pedestal, and reflect current demographic trends. Or, as a few are now beginning to do, they're going to have to consider the real-age health of those they are insuring, since a healthy seventy-five-year-old travelling the world is undoubtedly a better insurance bet than some grossly overweight person half that age. George Orwell once said something to the effect that fashionable writers tended to be under thirty years old. As a further example of ageism, George Orwell's remark, sadly, still holds true today. Chick Lit rules, and there are lots of examples of so-called Geri Lit being mocked in the press. Why should this be, given the age range of many book and magazine buyers? Look, for example, at Britain's *Saga Magazine*, which, aiming at the over fifties, sells well over three-quarters of a million copies every month. That's more than the circulation figures of most of the laddish magazines put together. With countries throughout the rich world growing demographically older, that type of unrelenting intellectual and cultural blindness is going to have to change its focus. We have spent centuries trying to find out how to live longer. Now that we manage to do so, it seems that the rest of the world still fails to acknowledge that change.

IS IT ALL OUR FAULT?

'Forty is the old age of youth; fifty is the youth of old age.'

– Victor Hugo

'We live in a decadent age. Young people no longer respect their parents. They are rude and impatient. They inhabit drinking taverns, and have no self-control.' That's no contemporary complaint: that's an inscription found in a six thousand-year-old Egyptian tomb. As the other old saw has it, 'The younger generation are alike in many disrespects …' There's little new around on that front either. Age historically disapproves of youth and youth replies by ridiculing age. We're not going to emulate any of that here, so no attacks on youth culture as such. We have to make our case without picking too many quarrels across the great divide.

As there are so many differences between the generations, some ageism is always going to be around. It's not just the years that separate us: it is our attitudes, the rapidly changing norms of contemporary society, and the different experiences, brief or lengthy, we have all had to face. Across the centuries, for example, people have always believed that past times were better. We think we remember our own youth and that we were much more respectful to adults than the young of today. But these things are almost certainly fictions, erroneous bits of baggage which we'll return to dispute later. While there's no age limit with regard to ambition, we also tend to believe that good judgement only comes with maturity. Unfortunately, while we are only young once, and old once, some of us can remain immature for ever. Nonetheless we believe that if youth ignores the vast experience of the old and all those other valued provisions we have brought with us through our lives, they'll suffer the direst consequences. That too can make a pretty thin case.

Perception between the age groups is key. We of *The Trailblazer Generation* may be proud of what we've done, but we can't rely on being famous for what we're going to do. If we pour a glass from a bottle of vintage Mouton Rothschild, we expect the very best, but not all vintages are great by any means. Victor Hugo wrote about the fire in the eyes of the young and the light in those of the old, but it all depends on our vantage point. Yes, we are equally guilty because we tend to see youth as a disorder which they will eventually grow out of. As we grow older, our memories become more sharply defined, but this, to younger people, just makes us appear more rigid, critical, fossilized, and opinionated. To those of our own age we may by contrast seem healthily conservative, dignified, tolerant, patient and understanding of the frailties of others. All those things add flames to contemporary ageism.

SAGE AGE

Most importantly, the young ought constantly to be reminded that being old does not signal that we're entering the departure halls of life. There are so many positive things over which the generations can and could assist each other even though the young inevitably have totally different time horizons. Death, pushing up the daisies, is a distant rumour to them so it is hardly odd that in their twenties and thirties they have very different views on life. They don't want to forego instant gratification, and, for example, will indulge in a major shopping spree rather than worry about their future pensions. We ourselves did exactly the same in the past when we would have been much wiser to start putting aside more cash in our early years. Ten, twenty, thirty, forty years ahead, soon becomes today. It's so easy to pigeonhole the future, but procrastination catches up with us all in the end. Youth has its sell-by date too.

Not unnaturally, the young have other different attitudes and aptitudes. They tend to have more enquiring minds; they outstrip us on that front since they have had less time to acquire knowledge. Their brains contain or demonstrate what is known as 'fluid' intelligence, which means that they adapt and learn in a much more agile way than we now can do. On that front, they easily outshine age, but there is another type of intelligence, that is born of experience. It's termed 'crystalline', a process where current problems and opportunities are assessed on the basis of past events and outcomes. Here older generations normally win the race, since a prior knowledge of what is likely to happen in any set of circumstances, comes to the fore. To test this out, Cornell University recently polled three age groups, of twenty-nine-, forty-four-, and sixty-five-year-olds. The questions put to those three groups all concerned life-skills and the solving of practical problems and disputes both at home and at work. A group of twenty-four experts analyzed the results, and the oldest age group came out on top in terms of finding effective solutions to the problems

'Life should begin with age and its privileges and accumulations, and end with youth and its capacity to enjoy such advantages.'
– Mark Twain

they had been set. These results clearly show that age and wisdom go hand in hand. Not unnaturally, however, the movers and shakers in contemporary public life tend to opt for the 'fluid' rather than the 'crystalline', thereby depriving them of that essential factor: experience.

In no way are the elderly, any more than the young, a homogeneous group. Inequalities among us are legion. While common problems might realistically be seen to bond those of us of a similar age, in practice huge differences extend into later life. Age is never a universal leveller. With the sharp decline in semi-skilled or unskilled jobs in most western societies over recent decades, this has inevitably led to mass unemployment or forced retirement in the areas affected. Those elderly people show just as many inequalities on a class or other basis as young adults. They tend to age prematurely and die younger. If we are rich, however, we manage to keep control over our lives for many more years.

Old? Yes. Obsolescent? No! The European Employment Directive (please don't yawn: it is important!) comes into force in October 2006. It will ban most forms of age discrimination in the workplace, something that has been the practice in most of North America for several years. Throughout the West, business leaders continue to oppose such moves, most employers wanting to retire people at a maximum of sixty-five. A compromise between that age and seventy is being widely debated in many countries, but in the meantime discrimination in the workplace is rampant. In principle, in most developed societies, workers are supposed not to be forcefully retired when they hit a certain age. But as an example, over eighty percent of a group of over fifties recently polled in London claimed that they had experienced either outright ageist discrimination, or total rejection by current or prospective employers. All this underlines a further imperative: there has to be a rapid re-evaluation of the age-to-work ratio in the face of current western demographic trends.

How else can we challenge the worst cases of ageism and age discrimination? How can we change the political agenda? These are some of the issues we need to get worked up about, and in a big way. One way not to react, however, is by emulating a striking feature of contemporary life in Germany. A report from Berlin in October 2004 announced that they were going to be forced to build a prison catering exclusively for pensioners. There has, apparently, been a 'grey age' crime wave, and the new prison will be built near a hospital and will have wheelchair access, since offences committed by the over sixties have increased by around twenty-eight percent in the last decade. In the same year, police arrested one gang who had committed armed robberies that had netted them nearly half a million euros, in order to boost their miserly pensions. The three-man gang were aged between sixty-three and seventy-four. Now there's an ageist initiative for us to think about.

THE GREY VOTE

'I will not make age an issue in this campaign. I am not going to exploit for political purposes my opponent's youth and inexperience ...'
– Ronald Reagan on his presidential challenger, Walter Mondale

The answer to all this is to press all the political buttons available to us. Governments and policy makers tend to be blinkered in their attitudes to such matters. They only see the problems: health, pensions and so on. When do they ever take account of our successes and achievements? And our potential power? The 'Grey Panthers' in the United States fight segregation against the old. We in western Europe lag far behind, though there are an increasing number of pensioners' organizations and other pressure groups which are beginning to make our concerns heard more clearly.

This leads directly on to how *The Trailblazer Generation* votes. At election times, politicians in most western countries talk a lot about mobilising the Grey Vote, but in practice do very little to cater to it. In the United Kingdom the over fifties comprise only forty percent of the electorate, but they are the most politically committed, and account for well over fifty percent of those who actually vote. Looking at it another way, Britain's over sixties are twice as likely to vote as its under thirties and these statistics are reflected in many other European countries. That should matter to all politicians when they lobby us over health services, street crime, pensions, winter fuel payments, free TV licences for the over seventy-fives, local tax reductions, and other bribes for *The Trailblazer Generation*.

We seniors know we've reached political maturity when we don't vote *for* a candidate or party; we vote *against* them. We know what we don't like, and who we don't like. At last we've started to make much more noise about it. The Age Quake has arrived. Against it and the backdrop of ever decreasing birth rates, we golden cohorts should be becoming an ever greater force in political and social life. If the voting percentages mentioned above don't offer a lot of electoral power to get up and change things with, it's difficult to see what can. It's up to us. Whether we veer to the left or to the right, more power to Grey Power!

The older we get, the more we should support the governance of a country with our senescent wisdom. Now there is a gentle word: *senescence*, which is a whole lot more comforting for those who have arrived here than, say, 'dotage'. Governments of all complexions are gradually being forced to find new ways of accommodating the aspirations of those of us once deemed too old to be politically active. But they tend to be a bit like advertisers; they believe that we always go for the same product. They also believe we're much less likely to change our voting patterns as we age. The results of opinion polls show that that so-called fact is also a nonsense. *The Trailblazer Generation* changes its mind too.

WORLD ATTITUDES TO AGEING

Here's a statistic we left out earlier on. According to the United Nations, the over eighties in the developed world are the fastest growing sector of the entire population. But each country, culture or society has remarkably different attitudes to ageing and to when a person is defined as old. Even in the more affluent nations, where many people want to carry on working after what is their traditional retirement date, preparation for it also varies greatly. Other UN research has found a remarkable degree of unity throughout the world for having a mandatory retirement age.

A recent international survey shows that Canadians and Americans have the most positive view of older age groups. They encourage a healthy reinvention of individuals in their later years. Japan and France tend to lag behind, but for different reasons. The French don't consider people old until they are well into their seventies, while the Japanese think that old age begins at fifty. Being old in other Asian countries can sometimes be advantageous, compared to the attitudes which prevail in the West. Many of us used to associate a gerontocracy almost exclusively with the People's Republic of China, where Chairman Mao, for example, ruled well into his eighties, and some of his successors have done the same thing. Maybe it's because the older you grow in China, the more you spend time trying to keep fit. From crack of dawn, the gardens of Beijing are full of the elderly going through their *tai chi* or similar activities. As one result of this, it's estimated that by 2040, the over sixties in China will have trebled to a staggering four hundred million! As an aside, in support of that ethnic group's great care and respect for the elderly, a young Chinese man was recently spotted helping a very bent Chinese grandfather along a Soho street. Passing observers thought, 'How kind of that young man,' and still thought so as they saw him help his very unsteady relative through the darkened door of a strip club.

In Japan many men retire in their fifties, but there too age is venerated much more than in the West. Living alone in old age is an almost fashionable thing to do there. But there are exceptions. In Japanese traditional theatre, for example, some of the male and female stars keep on acting well into their eighties. And don't let us forget Singapore, over which the powerful Lee Kuan Yew ruled for more than three decades. He still sits in their parliament, though he is well into his eighties, acting as a 'Minister-Monitor', watching benevolently over the young.

The French are somewhat better at dealing with age problems than the British. Most importantly, it happens in French political life. President Chirac is in his early seventies, and commentators currently see him standing again when his term ends. His predecessor, President Mitterrand, was seventy-nine when he finally left office. As another example, French television, in early 2005, was accused of blatant ageist discrimination. But on this occasion it was young stars and presenters who were angry that many senior presenters, some aged between sixty and eighty, were still dominating the news and variety shows. One of France's best known pop stars, Charles Aznavour, still captures audiences though he is well into his eighties. Such practices continue quite simply to ensure that the relevant channels capture an increasingly elderly viewing audience. As the head of TFI's news channel protested, their wish is to cater to 'people with a past by people with a past'. He believed that the age of the presenter was a distinct asset in this regard. Having acquired celebrity status over many decades, ageing celebrities stay on because older viewers require the familiar, and continue to give them top ratings. It's a great argument.

Where else do we see such attitudes in Europe or North America? In Britain there are almost no political leaders of any serious age. Thankfully, experienced people of maturity, who have now left the unpleasant limelight behind them, are still influencing the young decision-takers from behind the scenes, or in the House of Lords. Similarly, on television, there was an ill-thought-out tendency to get only pretty boys and girls to read the news bulletins. With a few intelligent exceptions, they were unbelievable. We saw them reading the words in front of them, but we realized that most of them had never experienced the sorts of stories they were commenting upon. It is like that long-term American saying: We don't believe the news until we hear Walter Cronkite reading it. Happily things are changing on that front as well.

With some of these notable exceptions, Europe lags behind the United States in recognizing the power of age. There are, however, an increasing number of important lobby and other pressure groups for the older generations coming into prominence. In the United Kingdom, the Third Age Employment Network, for example, lobbies actively against age discrimination, as does the National Pensions Convention. But British age-related lobby groups are still in their infancy in comparison with their powerful and well-financed counterparts in North America, where 'Intergenerational Equity' is a slogan we hear increasingly voiced. America has hundreds of extremely active pressure groups and lobbying organizations, not all of them based in what is disparagingly known as the 'Senile State', i.e. Florida. Throughout the United States, where the statutory retirement age is sixty-six, they have many powerful bodies such as the American Association of Retired Persons, or AARP, which campaigns hard and successfully. State and federal politicians are forced to listen. They know these organizations command many millions of votes, and everyone from the president down recognizes that such groups cannot be alienated. The British and others in the English-speaking world are having to run hard to catch up.

Given our huge numbers, and the financial and other resources over which we have control, where's all this leading? For a start, there's absolutely no doubt at all that more and more 'grey' political parties, or wings of existing ones, are beginning to emerge, as we come, belatedly, to realize how much we can change the issues that affect us. We discussed pensions earlier. It's an issue that keeps on returning to haunt us. *Pensions a Go … Go …* ran one recent *Financial Times* headline. It argued that, in the half-empty goldfish bowl of public life, the older fish are meant to grow larger because of the size of their financial bowl. One of the myths arising from all this is that we, the ageing population, will very soon have to be totally under-written by a dwindling band of taxpayers. The obvious reaction to all this is: and why not? We paid; now we play! Yet media commentators go on and on about how, pretty soon, *The Trailblazer Generation* will be draining all the nation's resources through state pensions and healthcare, leaving the young sucked dry by trying to fill the financial gap. Much of the debate is party-political and ideological, rather than accurately financial, more's the pity. It's all a bit like the crass suggestion that death is a handy way of ensuring that the social security system doesn't get overstretched.

POWER AND PREJUDICE

Senior citizens keep the economy going through their affluent spending patterns? Argue and discuss. There's a lot of rubbish going round and round questioning that general line. Yet recent statistics show that, far from the old sponging off the young, many of the latter age groups still live with, or depend heavily upon, their parents. They do so well into their thirties, or even their forties. They do so even if they are married, because it's cheaper, and because of rocketing house prices. They are known as 'Kippers', in other words, 'Kids in Parents' Pockets, Eroding Retirement Savings'. There's another cohort in American society, which the *Wall Street Journal* calls the Coddled Ones. They are the millions of young people between eighteen and thirty-five who also continue to live with their parents. The Italians and Spaniards who currently write a great deal about this category, call them the mammas' boys.

As we have seen, women still tend to live some years longer than men. Another gender specific picture has been built up in some recent media coverage, of the young suffering hardship while golden-olden ladies gaily squander the national wealth by having regular face-lifts, and living it up wildly in their eventide homes in Spain. By contrast, it was Nancy Astor who, in her vintage years, said that in her youth she was always worried that getting older would stop her doing lots of exciting things like travelling the world. Now that she was older, however, she did not want to do any of them in any case. That's a more mature argument.

PAPER WARS

Back to the so-called Age War. Young journalists writing about age will eventually change sides. We of *The Trailblazer Generation* feel that they tend to come to many annoying conclusions. As they grow older, however, they will begin to realize that we have become wiser, or that we have learnt more as they have gained in years. Yet still that serious gerontophobic culture lurks around in some sections of the media. Of course age conflicts are reported on when news stories crop up about businesses failing because tough new managers have to wait too long to fill dead men's shoes. It was the same when we were young. We too waited irritably to step into old brogues. We could not wait for elderly bosses to retire. It's not as bad as it is in Germany at the moment, where there's actually a political campaign group called 'The Right of Future Generations'. Their slogan is *A band of pampered pensioners is stealing the future from us!*

To some media commentators, some countries are in danger of becoming two nations: not in Disraeli's meaning of the rich versus the poor, but of youth versus age. These arguments again largely reflect estimates of rising life-spans and falling birth-rates. At their most extreme they suggest that in fifteen, twenty, twenty-five years' time, the nightmare scenario is of western countries not being able to afford its older generations, which will totally destroy society as we know it. The Great Pensions Gap Scenario is riddled with such fictions.

Back to Germany. There's a true story that, back in the 1870s, the then Reichschancellor, Otto von Bismarck, was asked to rule on when government clerks and other civil servants should start receiving their pensions. His immediate reaction was to ask his advisers by what age most of them were dead. The blunt reply of 'sixty-five' set that as the pension age. When Sir William Beveridge outlined his ideas for universal state pensions in Britain in 1942, the future life expectancy for men was estimated to be the early to mid sixties. Which is why the UK still has their public sector male retirement standing at sixty, and for females, at sixty-five.

The campaign to raise the British male retirement age from sixty to sixty-five or even seventy, with higher state pensions offered to those who delay claiming them, is one that is bound to win in the end. On the other hand, as we discussed above, labour unions continue to argue that it's all a nasty, vicious plot. Keep people working till they are seventy, and Bismarck's ambition will be universally achieved. This is particularly relevant to manual workers who, they argue, cannot be expected to keep labouring until that age. Similar arguments are currently being fought in France, Germany, Italy, and almost every other western country. Who is right and who is wrong? Suffice it to say that it is screamingly obvious that few people can or will be able to create enough wealth in only thirty to forty years of working to support thirty to forty years of retirement.

The cult of youth automatically creates an implicit ageism in any society. There is nothing wrong with such a culture, but it should not be permitted to lead to age discrimination. We need to fight any and all gerontophobic attitudes. Many of them are, however, our own fault. We were once in charge. We let it happen. Creating a new brand for ourselves by using our crystalline intelligence is hugely important to all our futures. This has to be advanced by promoting Grey Age Power everywhere, from the voting booths to all areas of political and public life.

CHAPTER SIX

Been There, Done That

'Yea, from the table of my memory
I'll wipe away all trivial fond records,
All saws of books, all forms, all pressures past
That youth and observation copied there.'
                              Shakespeare – Hamlet

One of the greatest novels of all time is Proust's *Remembrance of Things Past*. The tag line for this chapter is the direct opposite: *Remember the Future*. Forwards not back. Right now that's much more crucial. Think hard about what is yet to be. Spending too much time looking back on life is like staring into a bowl of half-cooked minestrone: some parts have blended into a mush; other parts have stayed resolutely apart. Or maybe it's more like the difference between a broad-brush oil painting and pointillism: major aspects completely disappear into the background, while a few ancient sparks shine through. We grow older by the minute if we spend too much time living in that past, but we still have to pull it along behind us or go crawling back to it from time to time.

Seneca actually said it before Shakespeare. 'Life is a play,' he wrote. 'It's not its length but its performance that counts.' As we move about the stage, unless we meet with some fatal mishap on our way, we are bound to reach the last two of the Bard's seven ages of man in the course of time. Trotsky wrote that old age was the most unexpected of all things that happens to a man. Having read this far, most of us will agree that it's almost inconceivable that we've reached the age we are. How could it possibly have happened so fast? How are we going to cope? How are we to avoid putting on our mental cardigan and worn retirement slippers? How do we go about recreating ourselves without dragging all the past with us? In trying to destroy the old taboos about ageing, we mustn't go into denial. It's wake up or seize up time. There is only one future for us and it begins here.

NOSTALGIA RULES

'Never ask why old times were better than ours: a fool's question.'
– *Ecclesiastes, 7.10*

But what on earth's wrong with a bit of reminiscing? We all tell stories about our history to inform, entertain and amuse, just as in primitive societies the elderly pass on the histories and traditions of that society to future generations. What's wrong with reviewing one's past life from time to time? We can surely learn a lot from it. The answer is that, comforting though it may be, it needs to be kept under control. It's like telling the same old story two or three times to the same person. Don't become obsessive about the days of yore. Don't keep talking about all the wonderful things that happened back then. Most of them didn't.

OK. Let's think back to our youth for a moment. What was it really like back then? The Second World War and its aftermath dominated so much. When we grew up in the forties, fifties and sixties (and if we remember the sixties, as George Harrison said, we weren't there!), things were all so very different. Sweets and junk food were less available, restaurants were fewer, television and the tabloid press were not all-dominating. But so many old remembered things never happened and never were. Our bad memories create the image of the 'good old days'. For example we bemoan the lack of the little corner shops that once were everywhere. We forget the narrow, monopolistic choices they offered us as compared to the huge and competitive range offered in today's supermarkets. We remember that trains were always clean and ran on time. That too is total nonsense.

Nostalgia ain't what it used to be. Of course there's absolutely nothing wrong with a bit of pondering over our past hinterland just so long as we don't muddle it up with old longings. They tend to bring melancholy or bitterness in their wake. Nostalgia can, when appropriate, be a pretty harmless pastime, and doesn't necessarily bring gloom with it, but here's the rub. Avoid the all too common failing of being weighed down by a boatload of missed opportunities. Bewailing what might have been is not the best way to confront the future. We can't drive our lives forward if we're always looking in the rear view mirror. Steering ourselves in that way can lead to people around us thinking that the future doesn't matter to us, or worse, that our short term memory is failing fast. As to the future, the most important thing to realize about it is that it doesn't yet exist. So we can help make it.

Come off it! What's so wrong with wandering down memory lane? Nothing wrong with a lane, but if it turns into a motorway, we can land in dead trouble. Yes, we're only what the chain of memory tells us we've been. Yes, we know nothing without it. Yes, that's the bluntest of all facts. Yes, one bit of good news on that front is that if we've a bad memory for faces, we meet new people every day! And why not when even the young go around with their poignant nostalgettes: 'What an amazing time we had at Glastonbury last year!' a junior repeated last night. We'd heard that before, many, many times. So another thing we must all stop doing, particularly when our descendants are hanging around us, is whingeing on and on repetitively about the good old days. Memories are old; opportunities are new.

No matter how hard we try, we still slip backwards rather than move forwards. We continue to recall all those past chances we seized or missed. We remember the tipping or turning points in our lives which totally changed our ambitions or directions. If we hadn't gone to that pub or that party, we wouldn't have met that splendid 'significant other' (dreadful expression), who totally altered the uneven tenor of our ways. A chance

conversation, a missed train, a whimsical desire to take a holiday break, logging onto some odd website, underlines the fact that it was 'events' we learnt to be wary of and most respect.

From now on it's going to be future events that matter. In any event, large tracts of our youth, and of our adult careers, are best left alone and unvisited. But no matter how strong-willed we are, we'll continue to meander back to those unhinged opportunities and mistakes we made, but that seldom makes us want to live our lives all over again. Some of us may still feel the twinges of youth and exuberance inside our ageing bodies. Most of us would shudder at the prospect of having to relive our childhood, teens, twenties, thirties, or forties all over again. So set aside the old shibboleths. Unhitch the memories, park them in a siding, and we can go harmlessly back to them when we've prepared for the future. Let go too the greasy pole of past ambitions. That glory was fleeting, but obscurity is for ever. The past has gone, so try to put aside all its little triumphs and tragedies. We can dip into that pit a little later on when we've unearthed the skills and experience we've gained, dusted them down, and started using them once again.

Minding what matters now, matters now. We did that stock-take of ourselves earlier on. The crucial test is how we're going use it to remodel our identity. In many people's view it's almost certainly the biggest problem we've had to face since adolescence. But that drags us back to the past once more, because we're still defined by little things that flatten our current identity. Our passport may read 'businessman' or something similar, suggesting that we've always been a cog in some machine, but life is more than that nowadays. We want to establish what our new status and position in life is to be. We need our history to help us. We don't do it deliberately, but we do it all the same, building up our glorious careers, junking the bad bits to keep ourselves sane or to attract respect or sympathy from those around us. Our experience is encoded, warped, pigeonholed, invented, polished, to suit our present mindset. Absentmindedness, the inability to retrieve precise facts, is something totally different, since we all have forgotten names, faces, numbers, and other convenient facts, from our earliest schooldays onwards.

ANECDOTAGE

One contemporary writer claims to have invented the word 'anecdotage', so the quotation from Disraeli is slipped in here deliberately to disprove him. In older age, the years become short and the days long. To build ourselves up, we reach our anecdotage, and reminisce to fill the days. Our best stories tend to get longer as we age. We do it all the time to embellish the present. Anecdotes, short and reasonably true reflections on human behaviour, are biographical devices that Churchill once referred to as 'the gleaming toys of history'. Like famous quotations, similar incidents appear to have happened to a range of very different individuals. Some books of humorous quotations seem to attribute half their contents to Oscar Wilde, Mark Twain, or Woody Allen. All these men probably did was rerun old, worn remarks in better coloured dresses. The British politician, Michael

> *'When a man fell into his anecdotage, it was a sign for him to retire from the world.'*
> — *Benjamin Disraeli*

Portillo, recently told an amusing story about himself and one of his constituents to about a hundred people at a lunch in Glasgow. They all went away believing that it had actually happened to him. He admitted later that it was a story that had been told about and by at least a dozen other MPs. A curse on all those who said clever things before we ourselves got round to it.

So even if we are hugely honest with ourselves and with others, our past lives tend to get edited, by the day, the month, the year. We think it makes us more interesting to our listeners. Mark Twain proclaimed that we all know for certain facts that are simply not true. The new word on that front is 'factoid', an assumption repeated so often that it becomes impossible to contradict, like the fact that Prince Charles goes around talking to plants or that every word George W Bush utters has been written for him. Fictions like that become fact. Fables embellish real experience. We may not always do it deliberately, because our recall system often acts like a badly behaved filing cabinet. Some things we will always deny, or bury.

It's like autobiographies, and not a few biographies, for many of the latter are mere hagiographies. Autobiographies are like carefully edited obituaries, with the final chapter waiting to be written. No less a person than a recent editor of the Oxford Dictionary of National Biography said that no really good story about anyone contained in his wonderful volumes, is entirely true. Or maybe, if we're writing our own life history for the benefit of our descendants, we'd be better calling them 'memoirs', with the good bits, the flattering asides, carefully weeded and entered, and the bad bits spiked. Or maybe, just maybe, when we start writing something down about the past, we see the value of not writing it down. Stages of life are blurred recalls of half-remembered events. Few of us keep anything other than engagement diaries these days; so much about events and people and places quickly becomes forgotten. We programme ourselves to bury the nasty items, filleting messy bits of history to suit ourselves, which recalls Churchill's other remark that 'History will be kind to me, for I shall write it.' History is only what we remember, or what Voltaire said were 'fables that have been agreed upon'.

MEMORIES ARE MADE OF …

An elderly lady stopped a man on a cruise ship recently. She was standing half way down a long flight of stairs between the main and the promenade decks, and addressed him in the same words as that old music hall joke. 'Young man,' she demanded, 'do these steps go up or down?' The man's wife tells him that he was so taken aback, and not just because he was addressed as 'Young Man', that he replied 'Yes'. The lady thanked him and went on her way. Does this mean the man was going senile too? Or the story of the man with one foot in the bath and one out, who asked his wife if he had washed or not. Or the man who stopped to talk to a friend for a while, and then asked which way he had been going when they met, because it would remind him whether he was on his way to, or from, lunch.

Why, when a young person forgets something, it's usually funny, while, when an older person forgets, it's tragic? Remember the oft-repeated music hall joke: 'There are many benefits of growing old ... pause ... but I can't think what they are right now.' When he recently announced his retirement, Norman Wisdom expressed another version of this. At his age, he said, you lose three things: memory and ... the other two things escaped him.

Time is what stops everything happening at once. We have our memories but we are only what we are now. Past success never ensures present or future success, and fame can be the beginning of the fall. It's like politicians, who, in the paraphrased words of Enoch Powell, no matter how famous they once were, in the end die unhappy and alone at home, forgotten shadows from the past. Or, more likely, in some forgotten corner of the local geriatric home, acting out all their old political battles. Instead, they ought to be getting out and about, buying a painting set, taking a course in plumbing, or making some money and happiness in some properly respected profession.

We hear it all the time, a version of that constant moan, 'I want to be what I was when I wanted to be what I am now: rich and prosperous, and with lots of quality time to do all the things I really want to do.' Come off it! Turning back the clock is out in any event. Why waste time in wishing? Or remember Shakespeare in *Richard III*; 'I wasted time, and now time doth waste me.' As we've already admitted, there's no particular harm in a little bit of quiet nostalgia now and then, for example when we meet up with old comrades. But if we stand round the well of memory the whole time we might as well jump in and sink without trace. To coin another horticultural phrase, use your experience to keep tending the walled garden of retirement until the first gin and tonic of the evening. But in future let a few weeds grow and plant some wildflowers too.

FUTURE PERFECT

Been there, done all that. We can't stop the clock ticking, but from now on it's not just a process of adding years to life, but about adding life to years. Some people hate the thought of retirement, or think of it as a bit of extra time as in a football game, or collapse into a state of dependency on others. Do not let that happen. Now it's time, not for indiscretion exactly, but for becoming much more relaxed about things, compared to how we used to be when we were clamouring for advancement up the slippery career pole. With care we can get away with being a fraction more eccentric or even slightly outrageous from now on. What's the point of being shy or inhibited at parties any more? Be eccentric, but be warned: the neighbours may not like it.

The philosopher's famous glass is still half-full, not already half-empty. Retirement should not be looked at as a problem, but if serious financial or medical problems come with it, or if one's home life is unhappy and work used to be a means of escape, then those serious issues need to be ventilated and solved. Unhappiness can also arise simply from not knowing how to relax. But pollsters have found that, on the physical side, three out of four people actually say that their health improves after they give up full-time employment. This is particularly so if we discover creative play areas in which to occupy ourselves. True, we may never learn to play the violin as well as Menuhin, but we may learn to paint better than him. Remember how well Churchill painted after he stopped running the country. He wrote that the young sow wild oats, but the old grow sage. Good point.

Creativity becomes increasingly important, and it needn't diminish with age. It's important to remember that, throughout our past lives, at least according to some psychologists, we've tended to use only about twenty percent of our total brain power. So we can easily digest more and more information on more and more subjects until the day we die. The ability to recall it all off pat can be a different matter. But that crystalline intelligence, the experienced and deductive reasoning that comes with age, gives us a composition of self-awareness and an ability to make judgements based on long and seasoned experience. While some modern businesses feel the need for nimble young minds and fingers to keep the tiger economies of the Far East at

CRYSTALLINE INTELLIGENCE IS NOT GOING TO FIGURE MUCH IN OUR CURRICULUM IF YOU CAN'T REMEMBER SIMPLE THINGS LIKE WHERE YOU PUT YOUR TROUSERS LAST NIGHT...

bay, a lot of others are changing their attitudes through realising that experienced managers, when they retire, take a lot of background knowledge with them when they go. More and more business leaders recognize the 'deep knowledge' that cannot be written down or handed over to younger successors. Many organizations don't realize how much background intuition and experience has been lost until it's gone.

Remember, ageing is no spectator sport. We all take part, and we all commentate on it as we do so. But the point of living is to keep on believing that the best is yet to come. We acquire knowledge or a trade for, say, the first two and a half decades of our lives, followed by four decades of sweat and toil. Then what? Perhaps because we dread what lies ahead, we go into denial. We don't think about it at all until it happens. What we have to keep putting way up there in lights is that some of the best tunes in life are played on old fiddles.

'I'm not young enough to know everything.'
– Oscar Wilde

Knowing how to grow old is a masterful skill. Don't get dragged through life. Walk! Yes, we're all hit by the typical realization that not only do all policemen look like boys, but so do presidents, prime ministers, judges and archbishops.

It happens like this. We haven't been paying attention. Then somebody plays the game, a version of which appeared earlier on, of asking each of us to look in the mirror and guess what age we are as if we didn't actually know the answer. We may see a face that reminds us of our mother or father peering back at us. That's why an unexpected snapshot taken of us can deal a heavy blow to the perception we have of ourselves. We're not alone if we suddenly realize, as we struggle to pick up a heavy suitcase, or get breathless when hanging a picture, that we're no longer in our youthful twenties or thirties. We see the number sixty-three, and think we've turned dyslexic; it should be thirty-six, surely? We look at the number of candles on our latest birthday cake, and think that they probably cost more than the cake itself, and that it's in danger of collapsing under their weight. The array of flames brings back memories of bonfires or having to call the fire-brigade. We have to recognize our physical limitations, but we're still not too brittle or frail to do anything new. We should hold our heads high and quietly repeat to anyone who is prepared to listen, but particularly to ourselves, that we know we still have a decade or three of highly productive quality time ahead.

GAP YEARS

'The afternoon of human life must have a significance of its own, and cannot be a mere pitiful appendage to life's morning.'
— *Carl Gustav Jung*

Look at it another way. Before they go on to university, or directly into employment, young people leaving school nowadays are increasingly encouraged to take a gap year. It's a rite of passage to enable them to find their feet in their struggle from adolescence towards adulthood. But it's many of us of *The Trailblazer Generation* who need some such time to help us bridge the gap we're facing. It was Lloyd George who said that the worst way to cross any such chasm in life was in two jumps. Yet so many people, claiming senior citizen status, are bewildered by it. 'What will you do when you retire?' was an unknown question in the past. It's a very common one nowadays. To help answer that question it's a matter of throwing away a lot of the old maps and buying new guides to lead us to our destination. As we move through our fifties and into our sixties, so few of us, apart from worrying about whether our pensions will support us, make any real effort to think about the huge emotional and practical chasm confronting us. Of course a large number of us can't wait to finish work. How often do we hear people say 'Me? Retired? I'm busier now than I ever was.' It's like those fridge magnets that read, 'How young can you be to die of old age?' or 'Retirement is when you stop living at work, and start working at living.' Trite, but not bad messages.

Increased longevity, yes, but in the end we all have to cross the river Styx since no one gets out of this life alive. It's up to us to adjust quite a lot of the timing on that. It's not all fun and games on the way, but if we plan well and establish healthy ways of living from our fifties onwards, happy and prosperous ageing is no oxymoron. We need to monitor what stimulates our wellbeing and what drives us to depression. We need to look for ways to cope with the sort of stress or hardship which lowers our defences against illness. Our good or bad physical and mental shape are factors we have to think about more and more. We know our chronological age won't tell us what physical state we're in. It's like an old house or an old car, or old underwear. The age of it can be irrelevant: it's how it's been maintained – and just think how marvellous some vintage cars are – that matters. We can be sick or well at any time in life. Some people we know seem prematurely dead. But we can be physically incapacitated in one way or another, and still be full of life, so trying to define what 'healthy age' is, becomes highly subjective.

The past supports the future. We write a sentence, think a thought, take some action, adopt some cause, then pause and realize that we did exactly the same thing thirty or forty years ago. History, our history, repeats itself. We worry that what is patronizingly called our second childhood may winkle us out as we travel through time, particularly if our memory starts to go. But if it is only Alzheimer Light that's nibbling at our Teflon brains (where nothing sticks), we mustn't get frightened. Yes, there are lots of jokes around like the man saying to his ageing friend, 'Are you thinking of taking another job, or studying for a new degree?' to which the reply comes, 'Hell no. At my age I buy day-returns and not season tickets. I think twice about buying green bananas. And when I order in a restaurant these days, they look hard at me and ask for the money up front!'

LAUGHTER AND TEARS

In this ageist world, despite the ever healthier ticking of the modern biological clock, many men and women are considered well over the hill even by the time they reach their early fifties. Apart from a few notables chosen to sit in the British upper chamber, the House of Lords, a place, as someone wittily said, that proves there is life after death, as well as some senior citizens found in the churches and the law (though in Britain judges now have to retire at seventy, and the world's Roman Catholic Cardinals are not allowed to gather and vote for a new Pope if they are over eighty), youth and inexperience, with a shallower hinterland, is put forcefully at the helm. Because we oldies are prejudiced enough to believe that youth has the cutting edge of a butter-knife, if we try to question this, we are attacked. Humour is always a better weapon.

Talking of biological clocks, isn't it a fraction odd that when someone retires after years of long and faithful service to his company, and although precise time-keeping will therefore be of much less importance to him in the future, they often present him with an engraved clock as a farewell present? Is he meant to stare at it till he passes away, in which case, would a sundial not be more appropriate? Or a wall calendar for that matter, to tick off his days? And would it not be a great deal more intelligent to have given a clock to him, or an accurate watch, at the beginning of his career, to ensure good future time-keeping? The answer is no. That clock is there to remind him to utilize the several decades left to him to best advantage.

Scornful, gritty, stand-up comics often fill their coarse-worded acts by mocking us, *The Trailblazer Generation*. They parade their grey-bearded jokes again and again. Many of these young humorists go around making it clear that in their minds the elderly are, above all, foolish. They may sometimes be right. But the elderly have conclusive evidence that the young are foolish. They too need to be mocked. In their repertoire they claim that age is when we oldies hold a really wild, wild, party, and the neighbours don't even notice. And here's very common joke number two. We tell a friend a really amazing bit of gossip, or a secret, and tomorrow they can't remember what it was all about either. Or some days we wake up feeling really rough, like the morning after the night before, but then we realize there wasn't a night before. Or we talk to old friends about our medical problems. That's known as an *Organ Recital*. Or benefit from the fact that when we're out driving these days, speed limits no longer need to be a challenge. And then they retail Lord Beaverbrook's advice (though, deep down, our longings may still be alive and well) that Old Masters are always a better investment than young mistresses. And, yes, we're even allowed to get angry at those road signs showing two decrepit people crossing, to indicate the presence of an old people's home …

Young mistresses … you wish! The sap of life retreats, and our steps begin to lose their spring. It's like the old excuse about impotence: that the bromide that they put in the tea when we were serving in the army is at last beginning to work. Ageist humour is OK if we tell it. It's very different if they do.

To repeat: retirement is still based on the ever more fragile myth that intellect and mental vigour diminishes rapidly from around sixty onwards. Wrong. The vigour bit, in particular, starts diminishing a good forty years earlier than that. We mustn't let ourselves become jealous of the past and its prowess. There's no point. The ambition that runs in our veins doesn't need to be replaced by the prospect of embalming fluid for a long time yet. Or by a wish to do nothing but spend more time on a golf course, which is more or less the same thing. Yes, many may disagree with that!

In summary, we need to learn to relax and forget about all the missed opportunities of the past. That's been this chapter's message. Don't spend time regretting the temptations we once resisted. Beware of wasting too much time anecdotageing. Remember the future instead, because minding what matters now, matters now. Bringing all our old skills with us, it's now time to better manage our health and welfare and establish our new identity and purpose. Youth may even respect us for it.

CHAPTER SEVEN

Ditching the Downside

'A man is not old when his hair goes grey.
A man is not old when his teeth decay.
But a man is approaching life's long sleep
When his mind makes appointments his body
   can't keep.'

                                                    – Anon.

Ripen before you rot. Wear out, don't rust out. These popular warnings prompt us to watch out for the perpetual flipside to life. It ain't a bowl of real cherries if the pips are lacking, and pips can break teeth. We reach across the toast and marmalade of a morning, and pick up the newspaper to reinforce our views on a wide range of topics. We fume and seethe at the stupidities of the world. That should be a red flag of warning to us. Stop and think. Remember, with once youthful eyes, the traditional reputation of the elderly, and beware! Grumpy old men. Bitchy old ladies. Grumbling, groaning, and complaining, and that's just at ourselves. Sadly, age can reinforce any bad habits we have brought with us through life. Tempers and sulks erupt or fester, though neither letting off steam nor nursing our wrath to keep it warm is usually of much benefit either to us or to anyone else who's around.

THE SEVEN SINS OF AGEING

Some retired people think they have become a burden to society. As we have seen, many of them live in the past and have too much time on their hands. They keep blaming external circumstances for the position they find themselves in. Instead, they need to readjust those circumstances to their own requirements. The world will walk over us if we lie down and let it.

The seven sins of ageing, culled from many sources including several groups of *The Trailblazer Generation*, are easily listed. They are:

1 Couldn't care less.
2 Can't be bothered any more.
3 Don't have time.
4 My mind is closed.
5 I'm in denial.
6 It's none of my business.
7 My ambitions are no more.

Adopting such attitudes will cause us to dread one day at a time. How much are they all to do with us having much more time on our hands? How much is it because of the frustrations of a sudden loss of status and an emasculated career? Answer: a lot. There's some well-researched evidence which indicates that a person's place in society's pecking order is critical to happiness and even to life expectancy. A loss of our past status is equally pertinent to our ability to cope with all the negative aspects of retirement, as we become what Turgenev referred to as 'the redundant or superfluous man'. Anything that adds to an increase in our self-esteem, can, by contrast, lead to a positive attitude to post-retirement living. One recently reported statistic actually suggests that optimists live, on average, nineteen percent longer than pessimists. How that was measured is unclear, but it's another good number to throw around as we move ahead. If optimists claim that this is the first day of the rest of our life, pessimists argue that this is the last day of our life so far. It's a truism: pessimists burn their bridges before they get to them.

Pre- or post-retirement, it's not, apparently, where we stand on the rich–poor scale that matters. It is more about how we're positioned relative to others close to us in the society in which we live. Feeling inferior can actually make us ill. Envy of others can also be a negative factor in conditions as diverse as cancer, heart disease and mental health. Alternatively, our personal autonomy, how much real control we have over our lives, can lead to increased longevity, and, crucially, to the happiness we all seek. Studies in Europe and the United States have produced very similar outcomes on this front. So we need not only to keep our self-control, but also control of our own homes and material possessions for as long as possible. When we lose them we begin to lose our identity. So make sure to maintain full control of everything from our finances to our wine cellar. The trouble is that our actions or reactions may slow down and, as a result, we may find that if we live surrounded by the young who realize that we're not responding quite as quickly as we once did, they may start trying to rule our lives. Let them and we deteriorate rapidly.

IDENTITY MAKEOVER

As we have seen, a constant intrusion by remembrance of things past can be hugely uplifting or life-destroying. If, in recent years, we've lived inside a protective bubble of achievement and success, we're suddenly going to have to face all outside problems on our own. Even if the fanfares of those past successes are still ringing in our ears, after power, or fame, comes the fall. Ageing is not an affliction, but there is no point in going into denial as a less certain future presents itself. To repeat, we can't drive by constantly looking in the rear view mirror.

But our sense of self-esteem can be recreated. A friend met up with a once-famous man recently. His name and picture had always been on the front pages of the newspapers or on our television screens. Now he was in a supermarket. He was shopping, alone, wheeling a trolley piled high with groceries and toilet rolls. He remarked that another customer had just recognized him, and had asked him, 'Didn't you used to be someone?' It made him think whether he had been. Then, as he reached up and took a packet of cornflakes from a high shelf, he added, 'There's got to be more to life than this'. He was joking of course. He had long realized that we are all only what we are today. He had created for himself a new, busy and profitable, but very different and low-key life.

Negative attitudes to life are definitely to do with the loss of the authority we once had. It can happen from one day to the next. No longer are we highly paid politicians, teachers, successful business leaders, or, indeed, policemen. Many famous names disintegrate rapidly without the oxygen of publicity they once had. Retirement inevitably highlights the downside of life. A friend recently called it his grimmest year so far, 'those last few days, losing my position, dropping down into the pit of retirement, no longer seeing my name in the papers.'

That sudden lack of command and purpose, and of being in charge, means we have to learn all over again how to deal with all the unexpected aspects of life. The value we once added to things now seems to be value subtracted. We no longer have a job title such as *Managing Director*. We no longer benefit from all the fringe benefits we once had. We realize this when confronted with the most trivial of things: how quickly, for example, the world's airlines forget their long-term loyal customers. When we travel, we no longer have Platinum or Gold Cards, and not even Silver, to wave at the check-in desks. The executive waiting rooms at airports are now denied us. Such little things encourage this sense of us as nonentities or has-beens. Life has shrunk, and what is going to replace it?

The German philosopher, Goethe, said that 'a man can put up with anything except a succession of ordinary days', which further indicates the dangers of suddenly having too much futile time on our hands. But now that we have stopped competing with others, we should be able to reassess people who are still out there in positions of so-called power. We see through them more easily, as we become less concerned with our own egos. Those of us who had a certain status and success in our lives should easily conquer those negative aspects and build anew.

OWN GOALS

We all know that better diets and lifestyles, which we'll discuss later on, can affect our attitudes to life. But continuing to act as decision-takers rather than the followers of orders, plus the handling of more intangible aspects like stable, happy marriages, all combine to promote better health and temperament. More choice, ambitions realized, and an absence of stress, are equally important factors. Some specialists argue over these issues, but there's no doubt at all that unhappiness, chronic anxiety, money worries, and having failed to advance in one's past profession, are highly negative factors in coping with post-work life.

Wrinkles on the skin are OK; they are the etched lines of experience. But don't let them invade our mind and soul. Wear a scowl and those wrinkles show up even more. The world has problems enough without us moaning. Finding fault with everything displays our own faults. Critics of others are self-appointed, and it's the same with temper. If we're right we don't need to show it. If we're wrong, we shouldn't show it. Bad temper, particularly over little things, is its own scourge. A lot of ill-tempered dross does threaten to explode with age, and it's got to be filtered or sieved off before it does some collateral damage. If we, the

SO YOU'VE BEEN AIRBRUSHED OUT OF THE PICTURE — THERE'LL BE OTHER DAYS, OTHER PICTURES — EAT YOUR CORNFLAKES AND GIVE ME A BIG SMILE...

silver-haired *Trailblazer Generation*, are to grow our place in modern society, that sort of negativity has to be swilled down the nearest drain. Ageist acerbity or plain grumpiness undermines our overall, long-term strategy. We must also not be seen to become too judgemental. Or mean. Don't be: we can't take it with us. Above all a sense of humour lubricates life. Try laughing. A smile, a happy expression, is the best clothing we can wear. If we can't, try wearing a paper bag over your head.

In previous chapters we highlighted many of the positive aspects of ageing. Ceasing full-time work can be a hugely liberating experience. Employers no longer control our lives and it's largely up to us to decide what we do next. But we mustn't allow ourselves to be airbrushed out of the picture by those around us, nor slip into self-imposed victim-hood. No blame-storming. No guilt-fests. Unfortunately we all tend to expect that the world in general will stay the way it was. It will not, and with all the good aspects come lots of downside risks. The relevant section of retire-ment's Highway Code points out a number of crucial warning signs we all need to beware of. Those who have been self-employed are more able to breeze hap-pily into a period of creative leisure. They can choose their own timing to do so. But there are millions of other veterans, who, for statutory or other reasons, suddenly find they are pensioned off. They know they still have so much going for them. They are not dead yet. Depending on their make-up, many of them tend, consequently, to respond to this startling change of circumstance in several different ways:

1   They accept their fate, then pick themselves up and do something constructive about it, or,
2   They sink into carpet-slippered dejection, or,
3   They get frustrated, and start hitting out angrily in all directions.

Having already addressed many of the challenges of options one and two, we now need to think ever more seriously about option three. If we play it right, age can be cool, wicked or stimulating. But then, in front of us, a number of those ugly warning signs appear indicating nasty potholes on what should be the tranquil progress of our lives. Exciting lifestyle choices are unexpectedly waylaid by unpleasant habits: all those seven sins of ageing mentioned above. We're bound to stand accused of some of them at some time or other in the future. They erupt, unnoticed by us, but increasingly recognized by those around us.

We've all seen it happen. Once highly agreeable, elderly friends or relations, become increasingly irritable and discontented. They sit in their armchairs,

metaphorical blankets around their knees, muttering or grumbling into their beards or tea cups. Unhappiness seems to weigh ever heavier on the shoulders. We should be wary of not following their unpleasant example. For example, everywhere we look, we think we see examples of the gross rudeness of youth. Swearing, spitting, yobbish behaviour, can easily build up into feelings that appear threatening to older people. Mobile phones being shouted into on trains and buses, pop music blaring from flats and cars, all add to the strain. Verbal abuse directed at us is not unusual, adding to the worries and uncertainties we have about our safety. No wonder, on the political front, yob culture is always at the top of the list of older people's concerns, even coming before financial and health matters.

Here is an up-to-the-minute example. Early on the day this section was written, as I went out shopping, I found myself getting angry, then wanting physically to remonstrate with a yob spitting disgustingly in the street directly in front of me. Then another, with a bad attempt at designer stubble sprouting among his acne, rode his bicycle straight towards me, in the middle of the pavement. I was tempted to take the law into my own hands, and try to stop him. Voice about to be raised, I thought I would explain to him, in the most basic terms, that he was a danger to elderly pedestrians and children, and that he was also breaking the law. I desisted, largely out of cowardice, since, examining him more closely, I realized that I would probably be the one to end up in the gutter. Besides, the question I should have been asking myself was why I was furious at his behaviour. Was it because, in my youthful days, my upbringing would not have allowed that sort of thing? Just then, round the corner, again in the middle of the pavement, came an old lady, speeding her way in and out among the crowd in a motorized wheelchair. Dylan Thomas suggested that we should not grow old quietly and calmly, but rage against age. I tend to disagree.

We know we are far from alone in wanting to act as law enforcers over the behaviour of others. We also know that we have to restrain ourselves. Why? Not least because, on an almost daily basis, we read stories in the media of the elderly being attacked, or dying of heart attacks, as a result of trying to act as policemen by attempting to stop some car theft or other act of vandalism. Though tolerance can come with age, the old don't always have enlightened views of the many indiscretions of youth, which we think of a disease from which we hope they'll eventually recover. Let's have a hard look at some other common *Age Rage* attitudes. Built on a foundation of frustration, they include grumbling, complaining, anger and intolerance. Railing against the world is not the most useful of occupations. And busy-bodying, if the problems don't directly concern us, is another thing to learn to avoid.

SLIPPING STANDARDS

It happens like this. The older we get, the more we tend to worry. We get irritated about little things. In the past, we would probably have merely frowned at displays of public expectoration or wayward cyclists. We would have ignored similar minor acts of vandalism as part and parcel of everyday sub-human behaviour. Now these incidents start getting us down. Why is this? Why do we repeatedly hear ourselves saying things like, 'It's all to do with declining standards among the youth of today'? Yet among the happy chain of memories of our own pasts, if we dig deep enough, we'll probably recall that we too got disgustingly drunk, misbehaved, and otherwise shocked the adults of our own early years. In those days, wow, did the neighbours complain!

Life is short but what is longer? It's also hard, but compared to what? Many of these bad habits are perceived to come with age. But most of them were actually nurtured in childhood. Carefully obscured in middle age, they are rekindled or reheated in later life. We can easily fall into the habit of complaining about a whole range of things. In reaction, the more youthful around us either fall irritably silent, tell us to stop, or simply ignore us. Then what do we do? We react by upping the stridency of our gripes.

In the past we could let off steam within one or other of the social tribes in which we mixed. But after full-time work, agreeable, like-minded colleagues become fewer in number. Losing such companions with whom we can quietly gossip or grumble, can lead to us withdrawing into ourselves. It's all too easy to become reclusive, not wanting to do things, go places, even on a shopping trip, or meet new people. But loneliness is not solved by shutting the door o'n the outside world. We need to build new relationships and to continue to network, by joining clubs and other interest groups. Gaining new, younger friends, as we lose older ones, becomes increasingly important.

But if our ambitions are merely to sit at a metaphorical window and watch the world go by, we need to choose one with a good view. A better solution could be to choose a street café in the sun. Forget Mark Twain's amusing but debilitating remark, 'Every time I feel a bout of energy coming on, I lie down till it wears off.' The road sign here should read: No loitering! No snuggling down in some mental ditch by the roadside waiting to die. Lethargy has to be fought off at every turn. We may get a bit bored from time to time, but we can always do something about that. What we mustn't do is become boring.

The Trailblazer Generation's frustrations are not always quantifiable. But a lack of positive activity easily leads to bitterness and discontent. Unless we are one of those oldies who decide to start paragliding at the age of eighty, an attitude that says, 'I can't do this any more.' can set in long before retirement. Keeping the mind active is essential, but physical limitations hit us all, as professional footballers, swimmers, even golfers, realize at some point.

GRUDGES

This is one of the other great sins of ageing.

I love to harbour my grudges,
Detaining them warm in my mind.
I like them to fester, my spirit to pester
Then I spill them right out when inclined.

I have grudges of every persuasion,
And hates that boil nicely inside.
Motorcyclists who speed; white vans that don't heed,
And my slow-lane progression outride.

My grudges are what keep me sane,
And fired up to such a degree,
They fuel my anger and upset my languor:
Do mobiles on trains hassle me!

My grudges are of varied dimensions.
They cause me the odd sleepless night.
They trouble my dreams with multiple themes,
As I fight with my recondite spite.

I revel in feeding my grudges
'Gainst my neighbours, my family, my friends.
With some ambiguity, they breed insecurity,
Which inflates my desire to offend.

I'm really allergic to mornings,
Why rise when it's raining outside?
I feel no attraction to physical action.
With inertia 'twould only collide.

I stand in the shower in the mornings,
And ablutions are far from my mind.
As I gently survey prospects for the day,
To activity I'm disinclined.

The radio news is concerning.
Wars and crises go right to my head.
Men never learn, but it's not my concern,
So I think I'll go straight back to bed.

I read so much about stress,
And my mind's in a helluva mess.
Should I laugh? Should I cry? Where do I apply?
Without stress can I be a success?

Without stress will I get out of bed?
Should I therapy take for my head?
For all that I read, I feel the real need
For a large gin and tonic instead.

— Michael Sinclair

Grudges tend to get locked away in the dark recesses of our minds. They re-emerge from the past when encouraged to do so. There are men and women from our previous lives whom, we admit, we could never stand. They are difficult to forget, but it can be well worth the effort. It is probably as much our fault as theirs. One such colleague met his antagonist at a party recently. When the man came up to him suggesting that bygones be bygones, fortified doubtless by the glass of wine my colleague had just drunk, he heard himself replying to the effect that 'I don't bear grudges, but in your case I'll continue to make an exception.' He turned and walked away, admitting that he had felt briefly pleased with himself and his acerbic remark. But not for long.

Despite our best endeavours, many of us dredge up occasional grudges from the past. The 'if only I'd played life differently' scenario, floats on the top of the septic tank of our past misfortunes. We think of those we liked or disliked, but especially the ones who thwarted our ambitions. 'I never wished a man dead,' H. L. Mencken wrote, 'but I have read several obituaries with a great deal of pleasure.' He's not alone in that. *De Mortuis nil nisi bonum*, the Romans said. But deep inside us we wonder why can't we speak ill of some of the dead, or begrudge some segment of our past if it deserves it. We have to try to bury such feelings since they can rot us. Or, to quote a Romanian saying, if we harbour grudges, in the end we have to dig two graves.

GRUMBLING

*'… And isn't your life
   extremely flat
With nothing whatever to
   grumble at …?'*
        – W. S. Gilbert

Then there's grumbling. We all do it. People who do it around us get on our nerves. Some grumbles we ignore since to challenge them merely leads to more explosions of the same. It can be particularly wearisome between partners. We step around a whole range of petty irritations like this on a daily basis. We don't even have to say anything to be known as a grumbler. A look, a shrug or a scowl, can replace a thousand words. Our companions know when we are angry, frustrated, non-verbally complaining. George Bernard Shaw used to say that you could always tell the English, because they could say the word 'Really!' in a dozen different ways. We all know that 'You're late!' can also be said in a huge variety of styles, from amused, to resigned, to real fury.

Grumbling takes the lid partly off some hidden sewer. It causes sadness and unhappiness to the grumbler and the grumbled-at. It achieves little. And the older we get, the more things we want to complain about or ban. The world, and a lot of people in it, is widely seen by us veterans as corrupt, confused, and inefficient. More than a few mature individuals we all know do nothing but moan about life's little difficulties. Many of us fall into that category ourselves without realizing it. If we're always bad tempered it's our fault. Medical authorities suggest that this can sometimes be due to high blood pressure and a host of other physical reasons. If however a bit of personal seething is tinged with some self-deprecatory humour, it can act as a sort of safety valve. Grumbling is an unfair accusation to throw around too widely, however. A sizeable majority of us keep our excellent humour and sparkle, living life as happily as we have ever done.

Some recent research for this book came up with some of the most common Age-Rage Grumbles, when a group of around a hundred senior citizens were asked what things they most disliked about contemporary life. Along with cyclists riding on pavements and expectorating hooligans, here is yet another list of major things they all tended to complain about.

1 The ill-expressed grunts and argot of modern life.
2 Graffiti.
3 Litter on the streets.
4 Chewing gum on the pavements.
5 Falling pension values.
6 Lengthy hospital waiting lists.
7 Modern pop music being played loudly.
8 Drivers of white vans.
9 Unknown celebrities being extensively written about in the newspapers.
10 Noisy neighbours.
11 Baseball caps.
12 Baseball caps being worn back to front.
13 Deliberately torn jeans, or baggy trousers trailing on the pavements.
14 Unshaven jowls.
15 Pierced body metalwork on men and belly-button jewellery on girls.

COMPLAINING

Selfishness, disguised by an expressed determination by many senior citizens not to be pushed or bullied, can emerge in later life. We can become seriously aggressive in our resolution not to be sidelined. If we look at some elderly people fighting for a place in a supermarket queue, or for a place in a crowded restaurant, or at the January sales, we often spot examples of such abrasive characteristics. For such people there always appears to be a tunnel waiting for them at the end of every light, yet they push and shove like mad to get there.

If we don't get what they want, we complain. That has several objectives: to get things off our chests, to seek retribution, to gain compensation, or, at the very least, to extract an apology. Before we do complain, however, we need to think carefully about how likely it is to benefit us or the world at large. When we try to act as unofficial policemen or litter wardens, this merely leads to unhappiness and lack of change. Many of our would-be complaints are best kept firmly under lock and key. Maturer criticisms have to be well thought out, rather than sounding like the whines of someone well past their sell-by date. There are lots of ways of obtaining justice without being branded as grumpy old gits, always singing the same broken songs.

Much complaining is born out of the worries we may have about the future. A famous Jewish telegram read, 'Start worrying: details follow'. We all have a floating list of worries that may, from time to time, keep us awake at night. We have probably had some of them for most of our lives. Money, health, career matters, family issues, all trouble us, even when there is little we can do about them. One solution is to list them all on paper, as we would with any professional problem, and draft potential solutions to them one by one.

TEMPER, TEMPER

*'I was angry with my
   friend;
I told my wrath, my wrath
   did end.
I was angry with my foe:
I told it not, my wrath did
   grow.'*
   – William Blake

Anger is only one letter short of danger. Watch out. In anger, which lies right at the high end of the danger list, our vocabulary tends to become very limited. It emerges like badly rehearsed theatre. Get angry and we immediately lose control of any situation, even if we are right. Some of us older people turn very bitter. As our teeth decay and fall out, we seem to go around biting more. Getting into the habit of constantly saying angry things (as we watch those dreadful young yobs misbehave or any current government mishandling things even more badly than they did in our young day) can be more than a bit off-putting to those closest to us. Turning ourselves into furious yobs wins no argument.

A friend goes spare when Italian waiters, serving him his meal, add the encouragement, 'Enjoy!' Such exhortations serve to irritate rather than inspire him. It is rather like Peter Ustinov's allegedly sharp response to the young man who wished him, 'Have a nice day', which was followed by something to the effect of, 'Thank you, but I have other plans!' Anger emerges from many sources. New frustrations creep into our lives and we find we cannot cope with them. A sense of impotence builds up inside us if we feel we are being conspired against. Such mental reactions tend to grow and fester. Frustration clones even more anger and that anger has to be defused.

INTOLERANCE

As we age, we tend to seek the familiar: courtesy, quality, politeness, agreeable music, habits, dress, and demeanour. When they are absent it's like a red rag to

'More often than not, the old are uncontrollable. Their tempers make them difficult to deal with.'
– Euripides

a bull. Brim full of intolerance, we deplore so many things. We construct verbal caricatures of those who surround us, or who cross our paths. No matter how broadminded we may think we still are, degrees of intolerance lurk inside each one of us. There's always some trigger, which, when pulled, leads to it erupting. The ventilation of outrage suppurates within us all.

We go around searching for remnants of the never-existent Arcadia of our youth. We don't want change. Or we do want change, but back to the good old days. We want conformity of behaviour, friendly policemen on the beat, well-behaved schoolchildren, and, deep down in even the most tolerant of us, a degree of social cohesion. We are no longer involved, so we react in more reactionary ways. Is there some rule that makes all men (and most women) grow more right wing as they get older? Yes, appears to be the answer, as age-related readership statistics of the more conservative newspapers around the world seem to indicate. It's a tendency that's been repeated throughout history. We cannot control things any more, so the state and others must do it for us. But being determined in our opinions does not make us right. We can be wrong. We should be alert to that fact as well.

YOUTH HANDLING

J.B. Priestley argued that when he was young, there was no respect for the young, but having become old, there was no respect for the old, so he had missed out both ways. He had a point. Old age needs a new mixer to make it tolerable. Veterans sometimes find it hard to talk to the young, because, they say, so little has happened to them yet. Quite often, however, it is their modern vocabulary or a lack of the elementary elocution standards that we believe we were taught, that acts as the barrier. We may think that the views of some of our own contemporaries are wrong or bigoted, but at least they emanate from mature cuts. What do we do about handling all this?

Youth, as we all know, inevitably thinks of the elderly as dated and set in their ways, though if we still have power or influence over them, that criticism will be muted. Behind our backs we stand accused of being old-fashioned and hypercritical of anything that's new. To prove them wrong, we have to stick to a number of well-established rules. We need to avoid being paternalistic or patronizing or too dogmatic. It's far better to establish their views first about whatever we want to criticize. Then we know where we stand. We can sometimes play the *Age of Maturity* card, since some young people like having gurus, and avuncular often can be good.

We may have to fight them off till we are ready to go. They all spend a lot of time, as we ourselves used to do, waiting for those dead men's shoes. Remember that de Gaulle said that 'the graveyards are full of indispensable men'. It's also useful if we are able to play modern, particularly the technology card. It's worth doing a bit of homework in order to keep up with the latest laptop or digital whatsit. What seldom works is the 'I was young once too' line, or 'I fell out of my pram worrying about that.' OK, so we too had loves, hopes and fears. The young are just not interested. And never forget that they may have the final say about our future. In all probability our own offspring will select our old folk's home.

Young or old, we tend to lose track of what is going on in worlds well beyond our age group. We note with astonishment that eighty percent of young people in Britain under twenty are reported not to know who Hitler or Stalin were, nor were they able to differentiate between World Wars I and II. Some of us may remember, from our student years, laughing at press reports about a notorious elderly judge who, in a court case, when the French actress in question was the most famous face in the entire cinema world, asking counsel, 'And who exactly is this Brigitte Bardot?'

Being deeply miserable, and a few seem almost to enjoy ill-health, is the only thing that keeps some people going. We should not be too dismissive of a gentle sadness at our own predicament. Self-reflection and self-deprecation, if amusing or sharp, can be quite creative. A bit of bile directed at ourselves from time to time can be a positive and regenerative attribute. Then there are all the significant behavioural oddities of those around us. We ignore most of them, or have got used to them, or don't notice them any more. Some are slight; some take a bit of getting used to: talking to oneself is a standard option, but there are lots of nastier ones.

Instead of all the negatives let's end this chapter on a happier note since, as Thackeray said, a good laugh is sunshine in any house. Here they are.

THE SEVEN CREDITS OF AGEING

1   I can be bothered.
2   I can still do it.
3   I keep my mind active.
4   I can create.
5   I can make time.
6   I deserve and get respect.
7   I still have my ambitions.

In conclusion, because we have lost our past status in life, we have to watch out for the trapdoors that tend to appear in front of us. It's so easy to slip into adopting a raft of potentially quite unpleasant ageist habits. No anger, grumping or grumbling. We often embrace such sins of ageing without noticing that we are doing so. Those closest and fondest of us will tolerate such slippage for a time, but in the long run alienation sets in and by then it's too late. It's all too easy to turn into a Saga Lout. Rectifying that is essential as we re-generage.

CHAPTER EIGHT

Twinges at the Hinges

'The secret of staying young is to live honestly, eat slowly, and lie about your age.'

– Lucille Ball

One way of staying young is to lie about your age. Life races on at a tremendous rate. The speedometer on the dial in front of us reads sixty minutes an hour. There are no brakes but there are some exciting gear shifts into which we can click the stick. But some problems won't disappear. Woody Allen, and a host of others before him, argues that we can live to a hundred if we give up all those things that make us want to live to a hundred. Another version of this, again attributed to Woody and several others, is that 'If I knew I was going to live this long, I'd have taken better care of myself.' We have only been given one body which is a bit like a portable plumbing system with lots of complex hidden wiring attached. Some parts remain strong, while others get blocked, self-destruct or ebb away.

We may even come to the point, we men that is, that when a girl says no, we're quite relieved.

'Grow old along with me! The best is yet to be ...'
– Robert Browning

To make a success of the future, recent somewhat conflicting medical research suggests that we've got to have started keeping fit at least by the time we reach our fifties. Why? Because that, they say, is the youth of old age. In the past, medical experts focused little on the lifelines of people of our maturity, since most people dropped dead before they got there. It's taken two hundred years to double life expectancy, and some gerontologists now argue that the true limits of the human life span may, in the not too distant future, lie somewhere between one hundred and twenty and one hundred and forty years. The trouble is that, in the meantime, medical science has improved so much that when a doctor examines us nowadays he's bound to find something that's wrong.

Ageing brings its problems, but there are so many consolations, as when, occasionally, the young even stand up for us on buses. We may occasionally try to stand up for a woman younger than us just to make an old-fashioned statement of politeness, but in this politically correct world, that can be seen as sexist. A friend did just that, and the young woman glared at him and yelled, 'Don't patronize me!' It was Max Beerbohm who said that most women are not as young as they are painted. We all, the old, the beautiful and the ugly, have one common enemy – time. It transforms everything. It is a one-way system. If they were still alive, Elvis would have been well into his seventies by now, as would Marilyn Monroe, and the sparkling young Diana, Princess of Wales, would be in her mid forties. Age shall not weary them, nor the years condemn. They don't grow older: we do.

'If you don't drink, carouse, and go out with loose women, you'll live longer.' 'Nonsense,' comes the hoary reply. 'It just seems longer.' The process of ageing affects all parts of our bodies and minds. A whole spectrum of degeneration is taking place the whole time, some of which is routinely repaired by our own inbuilt defence mechanisms. Our basic cellular structure also transforms itself throughout our lives, but our knowledge as to how or why is still far from complete. For example, we all experience body temperature changes from time to time which we cannot understand. Thus the commonplace remark, 'Is it me, or is it hot in here?' Many cells have their own fail-safe devices or may age at different speeds. They automatically ward off certain cancers and other nasties that attack the body. Medical science helps greatly by finding huge differences between individuals, so much so that 'elderly', or even 'very elderly', people can be capable of physical and mental performances that far exceed those of many young adults.

SEARCHING FOR THE FOUNTAIN OF YOUTH

Make-up can conceal age, but climbing stairs is a dead giveaway. Going uphill makes one realize how fast we're going downhill. Experts look at ageing or senescence from different points of view – biological, medical, psychological, and sociological. We age universally and progressively, but contradictions often arise as a result of interdisciplinary conflicts. Some specialists look on the process as an inevitable one of decline and deterioration; others try to stem the pace.

There are many publications to be found on futuristic hypotheses about the ageing process. The study of gerontology – the science of ageing – has made many advances over the years. On the fringes of science, however, in the meantime, we are promised amazing anti-age medicines and many other suspect treatments for rejuvenating people. Their protagonists tend to suggest that the fountain of eternal youth, the Dorian Gray effect, is there waiting for us just round the corner. Eternal life is still a rare commodity though some parts of the media seem to offer a prospect of it on an almost daily basis. We buy the jars of cream and watch, wait, and weep.

Among the sometimes rather odd guides out there in the market place about staving off the ageing process, one slim book that appeared recently goes on and on about the benefits of ginseng. Having dipped into it, one came to the almost immediate view that straight gin would be much preferable as the ultimate tonic (pun intended). Of course huge advances are being made in stemming nature's progress, but another example, in another publication, was of a young man being told that, in ten years' time, by following a certain treatment, his mother would end up looking like his sister. Now there's a thought! It all goes under the headline of 'working with science to keep you forever young', which is great news if it's going to work.

THE ETERNAL YOUTH SALES-PITCH

No one can slam the door on the ageing process, but there's a big industry out there selling us such dreams, deceiving us as to how we look, or could look. Sellers of make-up and cosmetics spend billions trying to persuade us that using their products can make us young once more. They may try, but we'll never get our youthful bodies or faces back. Instead we probably need to be courted by people who make trousers in beige with elastic waists, and slip-on shoes which may help disguise some of our frailties. We try to hide our shape and cellulite with underwear that looks as if it's been designed by an upholsterer. But the really good news is that more and more manufacturers are selling consumer goods and services especially for the elderly: gym equipment, spa memberships, exercise plans, trendy leisure wear, and health foods, as well as simply designed mobile phones and personal alarm systems. At one extreme there's even a bionic body suit for the elderly, designed in Japan and costing no more than a small car, which dramatically increases the strength of the wearer's arms and legs. Tiny muscle movements are transferred via sensors into serious muscular effort, and the stresses and strains of age are diminished as older people using it fend for themselves long into retirement.

If you can fake sincerity you can fake anything, said Laurence Olivier, but then you've got to hide the evidence of your guile. Way back in 1976, the Prince of Wales went on a grand tour of the United States. One engagement was a lunch at the luxury country house of a former American ambassador to the Court of St James. It was a most glamorous affair, not least because one of the distinguished guests was a very silent Frank Sinatra. He seemed to be in a world of his own, picking at the food on his plate but never putting anything into his mouth. It later emerged that he was on heavy sedatives, a fact confirmed by the dreadful red scars of a very recent facelift that ran bright scarlet around the back of his ears and behind his neck, just above the collar line. It was difficult not to stare at such a never to be forgotten sight.

"'How old are you?" he asked. "None of your business," she replied. "So act your age," he responded. She did, and dropped down dead.'

– Anon.

Putting aside the strategy of such surgical barbarism, there are other ways of trying to lie to the world about our age. We can always try to Botox ourselves young or have collagen injections or use age-reversal or de-crinkling creams. What else is there? Hair dyes and seaweed wraps? We may also have heard of lasers which nuke our wrinkles by stimulating collagen formation. But watch out; such processes can cause damage to the skin and the effects may not last all that long in any case. The actress, Kate Winslet, commenting on the current Botox craze, said that one consequence of it was that it was getting difficult for directors to cast women to play sixty-year-olds, since they all looked about forty. Not only casting directors but even gerontologists, confronted with sixty-five-year-old ladies looking fifteen years younger, actually admit in learned papers that even they find it difficult to guess at some people's ages.

We may marvel at those who are trying to join not *The Trailblazer Generation* but some sort of wishful Peter Pan club. We read with amazement how people queue up to buy longevity snake oils from the tailgates of some contemporary quack's wagon. We wait for all these exciting, life-prolonging things to happen, but then realize that the life we are living now will have to be enough for most of us. In any event, immortality could end up being that little bit tedious in the long run.

LONGEVITY LIVES

At a recent anti-ageing conference in London, a specialist from the American Academy of Anti-Ageing

Medicine suggested that genetic engineering, cloning, synthetic skin, artificial muscles, and so on, could, one day, extend the length and quality of life well beyond its present limits. Admitting that there was much controversy over his research, he argued that anti-ageing medicine was not a magic potion or a quick fix, but a detailed scientific approach. His focus was on preventing disease and body deterioration, rather than just treating it.

Another speaker, a British bio-gerontologist, was critical of much that was said at the conference, but still suggested that scientific advances could lead to an increase in human life span by some decades, adding that 'Many people here today are medics, interested in what we can do now: I am interested in things we cannot do yet.' Quite right too, though the social side effects of living well into our hundreds could pose a lot of problems for us in the process. Others argue that within the next quarter of a century, with the right amount of funding, we may be able to prevent ourselves growing old, or even begin to reverse some of the processes. If we can find ways to control certain key ingredients of ageing, including damage that occurs to our DNA and the build up of toxins in our bodies, some expect that within a few decades they will be able to hugely increase our lifespan. Others argue, perhaps more sensibly, that we shouldn't attempt to extend life beyond a hundred and should rather spend the money ensuring that our present lives become ever more healthy.

Longevity between species varies greatly, from the brief hour or so of life of some small moth or fly to the several centuries of the larger tortoises. It is not, as was once thought, all to do with bodily bulk: parrots and ravens live longer than many larger birds, and some fish apparently live to nearly a hundred, compared to the brief life of, say, a horse, at thirty years, or a dog at half that age. Like clocks, each species is wound up for a set length of time. But man's possible life span, long set in physiological terms at the absolute maximum of a century, is still very different from the average male life lived.

There are many quasi-medical texts around on other aspects of the human ageing process. Almost without exception, however, they seem to concentrate on fad foods, detoxing, the right vitamins, low calorie diets (since mice apparently live forty percent longer with them), fighting flab, extreme makeovers, and how to keep our hair, teeth, and toenails young and beautiful. On another route, researchers at Stanford University in the United States recently tried directly linking the blood supplies of young and old rodents. They found that the older ones benefited, and their progenitor cells were rejuvenated, while there was a decline in the younger ones' regenerative ability. Science fiction? Dracula, here we come. We can put mice to one side for now, but *Mens Sana in Corpore Sano* – a healthy mind in a healthy body – still has to be our overriding motto from now on. Keeping sane and agile are the two central parts of the ageing process most discussed by all those serious gerontologists who study our many symptoms.

FIGHTING FITNESS

'To get his wealth he spent his health,
And then with might and main,
He turned around and spent his wealth,
To gain his health again.'
– Anon.

Good health means that we die more slowly. Universal research has found, with almost no one disagreeing for once, that a reasonable amount of exercise remains a crucial key to longevity, whatever our age and no matter when we begin. Males between sixty and seventy who exercise regularly can end up as healthy on a number of medical scales as thirty-year-olds who never exercise at all. So we've totally run out of excuses for not exercising. The blunt fact is that members of *The Trailblazer Generation* are twice as likely to join the two hundred and seventy thousand people in the United Kingdom, with not dissimilar figures in most western countries, who have a heart attack each year, if we remain physically inactive.

That's the background. Now for some bright ideas, culled from a huge range of older people, about keeping our bodies fully active and healthy. Gravity pulls certain well-known bits of our anatomy lower as we age, but it's done that for many decades past. Some people seem to think that if we were meant to touch our toes at this stage in life they would have been placed further up our body. Neglect our physique and it gives up on us. Keep active in mind and spirit and the little aches and pains tend to take a lower place in our pecking order of worries, though, as we age, like a barometer, even the weather may start to affect our joints. From now on, general physical health has to be given a much higher priority than ever before, so let's begin by stepping out of the box we're in, and looking carefully at how physically competent we are.

The healthier we as a population have become over recent years, the more attention we have given to health matters. The biggest smiles on this front are that more and more of our body parts can now be replaced or repaired. It used only to be false teeth and spectacles. Now when hips or knees wear out, splendid spare parts can be inserted to allow for a mobility and a quality of life that was until relatively recently totally impossible. And think of life before modern hearing aids or contact lenses. Or heart bypasses, pacemakers, or motorized wheelchairs.

Before we turn to our *Mens Sana*, our healthy mind, let's cover a bit more groundwork on the *Corpore Sano*. We need regular help in monitoring the hidden physical wiring behind our ageing process. We don't want to go around with a visible health warning, neither in fact nor in appearance. But here's the rub. Our bodies, in the first instance, are not in the hands of consultants, general practitioners or nurses, but in our very own. We need the specialists to check regularly on how healthy we are, and an annual medical is a must whatever it costs. In that context, incidentally, it's a sad statistic that most health care costs incurred by any individual are in the year of their death. In the meantime, we need to remember all the flu jabs, eye tests, and prescriptions that are freely available to us. For all that, there's bound to be physical deterioration. Everyone is the same on that front, but many parts of us, and not just our waistlines, can be positively assisted by exercise and diet, which affects the pace at which that run-down sets in. But beware. Too much exercising can actually make one feel decades older, so take it gently. We don't want our family and friends getting their exercise by walking behind our coffin. On the other hand, if brushing our hair or teeth in the morning tires us, we really do need to get fitter!

DO OR DIET

Variety is the spice of life, but monotony buys most of the groceries. Some people commit suicide with a knife and fork, or, as the old proverb warns, we dig our grave with our teeth. The only trouble is that dieticians are like communist revisionists, undermining every previous precept. Once it was 'An apple a day'. It also used to be said that chips without the 'c' was what happened to one's figure. Now red wine is apparently good for us, and maybe those five portions of fruit and vegetables a day aren't as healthy as once proclaimed. So, one day, if this continues, mega pizzas may be back on the health menu, and it won't be as odd as it seems today to see very large individuals ordering double cheeseburgers, large fries, all washed down with, of course, a diet Coke. As the American said to the waiter in the French restaurant, 'No snails for me. I prefer fast food …'

Talking to friends of a similar age about one's physical ailments is (as we said earlier, but it bears repeating) known these days as an organ recital. Yes, aches and pains also tend to grow more frequent with age. We stoop a little more each year. Our senses of both smell and taste diminish in strength. Other bits of our bodies start to function less potently than they used to. We need to keep an eye on all those little things, like our sense of balance, and act quickly if any of them seem to get any worse. Keep walking tall. We're not yet heading for the River Styx.

'Is life worth living? That depends on the liver,' the old saying has it. And talking of liver and attacks upon it by too much claret or malt whisky, one old friend, a man of life-long broad girth, walks up to the top of the hill behind his house every morning, or round his orange and lemon grove when he's in Portugal, on the basic, medically argued, principle, that twenty minutes heart-rate-increasing exercise every day, at least three or four times a week, not just increases longevity, but allows him to consume a couple of stiff gin and tonics and half a bottle of something else every evening. He's proved his point … so far.

As further back-up to this point of view, at the corner of the Garrick Club bar one lunchtime, someone urged caution on the writer Kingsley Amis, who was already in the middle of his third lunchtime cap. He appeared to ignore the speaker at first, then stared hard at his glass, and said something like, 'Why would I want to give up all this pleasure in return for a few befuddled, incontinent, unremembered years in some eventide home?' The lawyer-writer John Mortimer is widely quoted as having said something very similar.

Abstinence is said to be a good thing, but it should only be practised in moderation. Eat well. Choose well. Live well. Churchill made some memorable remarks on that score. 'What's your favourite number at a dinner party, Sir?' he was once asked. 'Me, and a damned good head waiter,' came the rapid reply. On matters of cuisine, he would often say that he was easily satisfied by the best. And on the matter of drink, he was well known to have knocked back quite a few each day, maybe in the belief that it was not so much the cause, but the solution to most of life's problems. All that said, it's never too late to start eating in better ways, and not drinking too much since we all know only too well that a hangover is the wrath of grapes.

Too much alcohol? How much alcohol? How often do we see totally conflicting advice and evidence about how much we should be drinking? How many units per day or per week? Fourteen, eighteen, twenty, thirty? Then we were leaked that splendid news of the undiscovered benefits of red wine. How our hearts leapt when we were told. Remember that only a few decades ago it was Guinness that was good for us. So the red helps the heart beat better? Let's keep it flowing, as Churchill did when, at an ill-served dinner, he looked down at his empty glass, then raised it in a mock toast, 'To absent friends, coupled with the name of the wine waiter.' And forget too all the negatives behind the expression 'The last of the summer wine'.

Then there is tobacco. A decrepit old man was sitting on a park bench smoking one cigarette after another.

A curious woman started chatting to him and eventually asked him his age. 'Thirty-eight,' came the striking reply. At the other end of the social scale, at a recent diplomatic dinner in London, the American ambassador produced, at the end of the meal, a huge Havana cigar and lit up. It was politely suggested to him that it was illegal for Americans, particularly diplomats, to buy Cuban products. 'Don't worry,' came the elegant reply, 'I'm just burning the enemy's crops.' There are no excuses for burning such crops these days. Stopping makes some people put on weight, while continuing to smoke will probably put an end to more than our weight problems … eventually. Our ancestors had their excuses, since they didn't know about the dangers of nicotine any more than they knew about the hazards of breathing in coal dust or about asbestos poisoning. The only really good excuse ever heard for lighting up was the story of that crooked US vice president, Spiro Agnew, who was flying home from Washington DC one weekend, and found himself sitting in First Class beside a very beautiful woman. She, to his surprise, and it was still in the days of fully nicotine-fumed aircraft, was smoking a large cigar. Unable to contain his curiosity, he eventually asked her how long she had had the habit. The drawled reply went straight to the point. 'Mr Vice President, ever since my husband found a half-smoked one on the bedside table.'

FOOD FOR THOUGHT

How often do we see a healthy person in a health food shop? Butchers, bakers and greengrocers all have them aplenty. An ageing friend keeps telling us how many meals we've got left to have in life, adding that money not spent on good food and wine is money totally wasted. But as we age, and particularly when we can no longer take sufficient physical exercise, we may not need to ingest the same amount of food. But we still need the same intake of proteins and vitamins. And maybe we'll reach the stage when we can no longer cope with a binge-drinking night on the tiles. It is never ever going to be easy to get the balance right.

Sophia Loren said of herself and of her figure, 'Everything you see I owe to spaghetti.' When we read about diet, the advice we always get is to read the instructions on the labels. We never get as far as the small print. When we see a packet of peanuts, carefully turn it over, and on the back read the huge type 'WARNING: CONTAINS PEANUTS', we forget the rest of the detail. Or when we pick up a bag of 'Genuine, smoky, back-bacon, flavoured crisps', and it tells us that they are 'Suitable for Vegetarians', we tend to lose our patience. A favourite on that score is the bottle of Norwegian water bought in Bergen, which told the world that it came from the purest, million-year-old, glacier water. On the label it clearly stated 'Best before July 2005'.

BEND AND STRETCH

'I often take exercise. Why only yesterday I had breakfast in bed.'
– Oscar Wilde

Statistics show that the vast majority of people throughout the western world take hardly any exercise in their thirties, forties and fifties. They are much too busy career-wise. When they come home at night, dog tired, they persuade themselves that they've been burning up quite enough calories throughout the day. They tend to put on a lot of weight and don't do much about it. Later they come to regret it. However if they begin to exercise in later life they come to enjoy it, since they see such significant advances in their general wellbeing.

The more intelligent members of *The Trailblazer Generation* realize that exercise reduces the risk of heart disease and colon cancer, and also reduces our blood pressure levels and the dangers implicit in high cholesterol levels, quite apart from keeping limbs and joints in reasonable condition. Medical advice warns against any high impact activities, however, particularly if we're not used to them, so checking with the doctor first is the firmest rule. The most exciting up-to-date research from Australia on this front has produced growing evidence, from a survey of a thousand men with an average age of seventy-seven, that the more physical activity they undertook in their later years, the greater effect it had on their overall mental wellbeing, even including the avoidance of depression and the onset of dementia.

Most of us are in the same boat. We tend not to be marathon runners at sixty-five, seventy, seventy-five, or beyond. Though a few heroes do keep it up, we're no longer into skiing down the Eiger, nor sailing the Atlantic single-handed, though one woman in her eighties recently has done just that, with only one of her family helping her. Mountaineering or rock-climbing is better left to those who have always done it, and know what they are about. On that front, we read that even life-long squash players have to beware as they age. Doctors urge extreme caution with that game more than most others, because it puts a lot of sudden strain on the heart and it can also wear out all those fragile leg and hip joints. But swimming, walking, golf, tennis, cycling, at a pace to suit ourselves, places us way up there with the healthy angels in the medical profession's view of things. On the other hand, a man we know, having just finished a brief game of football followed by some very stressful tiddlywinks with two energetic five-year-olds, was left thinking about having a quick heart by-pass afterwards.

Can we put our trousers on standing up and still keep our balance? Do we sit down, or bend down, to tie our laces? As we will have discovered if we've got this far, this book bounces around with optimism. Where we come across unthinking, ageist attitudes, we attack. At one gym, and gyms are no quick fix unless we keep at it, on their exercise machines they had put up useful heart rate goal charts for different ages. Trouble was, those charts stopped at age sixty-five. What? No heart rate after sixty-five? There was a challenge. When confronted, the youthful management laughed a lot. They thought it was very funny. The member of *The Trailblazer Generation* concerned kept his cool, and said that he wouldn't argue, but that it would make a great story for the local press. They had taken the charts away by the time the gym member came back to cancel his subscription.

One thing gym fanatics argue is that, no matter what age we are, using weights is good for us, since it both increases our metabolic rate and keeps the upper parts of our body in better trim. On the other hand, pushing sixty is enough exercise for some and there's a common enough belief that we've hit old age when weightlifting and producing the odd beadlets of sweat means just standing up.

How about a regular return to the dance floor? What? Dancing? Yes, but we're not talking here about the old ballroom smooches and waltzes – the vertical expression of horizontal desire, as George Bernard Shaw called them – but highland or line dancing, and other modern steps. That tends to be more akin to gymnastics than to nasty old sex. Make it fun, but make it safe. Dancing in groups apparently can build up our bodies as well as our relationships with others. In Britain there's even a professional ballet group called *From Here to Maturity*, who employ dancers who are well into their seventies.

SLEEP PATTERNS

We've probably all heard Dorothy Parker's famous remark when she was told of US President Calvin Coolidge's death. 'How can they tell?' she asked. There is a similar story about the British Fascist politician of the 1930s, Oswald Mosley, describing the then prime minister of the day, Stanley Baldwin, as 'representing the yawn personified', or 'England asleep'. Catty lines can make good points. Some retirees seem to be determined to sleepwalk through the remainder of their lives, with few, if any, excuses for doing so.

Almost everyone's sleep patterns change as they age. Around a third of men and women over sixty-five notice this. Many older people have trouble sleeping right through the night and often wake very early in the morning. It's not that we need less of it but that we go in for shorter bursts of sleep rather than a straight eight hours a night. Sometimes it's to do with bladder problems, sometimes it's said to be the result of medication, sedatives, or the painkillers which we may be taking during the day. We older people also tend to start eating earlier in the evening than we used to, to get the initial digestion stage over with before we hit the sack. By the way, recent research proves that a fair amount of that exercising during the day also leads to better sleep at nights.

Some people from their earliest working years have always taken a brief nap when they could, sometimes lasting only a few minutes after lunch. Nowadays they call this *power-napping*. We wish we'd thought of that businesslike description at the time. Napping eventually turns into that most useful of words, the siesta, and, as we grow older, it now lasts quite a bit longer than a few minutes. Think of it in a more fundamental way: it's like breaking each day into two quite distinct parts. Perhaps it's a handy way of doubling our remaining life span, since many of us feel totally invigorated after that post-prandial nap. Even though we've yet to succumb to dozing in an armchair after lunch or over the television in the evening, that habit may be lurking just round the corner for all that we know. And no harm in that.

MIND OVER MATTER

Two elderly ladies had met for years to play cards. One day one of them paused during a game, looked at the other and said with

'Age imprints more wrinkles on the mind than it does on the face.'

– Montaigne

some embarrassment, 'Look, don't get upset. Isn't it terrible? My mind's going, and all of a sudden I can't for the life of me remember your name.'

The other glared at her for a few moments, then replied irritably, 'How soon do you need to know?'

There are many who write amusingly, wisely, and sometimes horrifically, about degenerative mental decay. We need to read and talk about it in order to recognize it. Memory loss often begins and is noticed by others, not so much because of the forgetting bit, but because we're seen to have stopped looking after ourselves as well as we once did. We stop eating regularly. We maybe drink too much, which certainly helps with the addling process. We start doing silly things with our finances, or wandering out on a cold night without a coat. Then, maybe, come the even odder things like getting caught carefully putting the shoe cleaning kit in the refrigerator, or the milk in the oven.

Our minds have to be kept active. The only mental exercise some people seem to take is jumping to conclusions about memory loss, and that's not always

very helpful. There is a massive amount of research around which is filleted by the newspapers, all pointing to the fact that those of us who keep our minds active and questioning, live much more agreeable and fulfilled lives. Consequently we try to keep up to date, though many of *The Trailblazer Generation* will inevitably get worried when, for example, so many of the names of apparently famous people written about in the newspapers mean little or nothing to us. It leads us to ask ourselves whether we are beginning to lose our marbles or whether it's because we're drifting into denial of youth culture in general. Are we stuck in a time warp, and does it much matter if we are? Are our minds going to sleep? And what of our memories? Let's give a few examples of the regurgitated research we're talking about.

Research in Canada in March 2004, reported on widely in the serious newspapers, suggested that learning to speak a second language doesn't just broaden the mind: it can, apparently, protect our brains against the ravages of time. Remembering that Canada is a bilingual country even though only eleven percent of the population speak both French and English, this research apparently showed that when bilingual people age, their brains decline much more slowly than those who only speak their mother tongue. Other aspects of mental deterioration were checked in older age groups, and it was found that they were more competent in all mental agility tests, they reacted more quickly to demanding circumstances, and they were less easily distracted.

A dear old friend rang up recently. Half-way through the conversation, she paused and asked, 'I'm sorry, I've forgotten. Who am I speaking to?' This is probably an example of something known as MCI, or Mild Cognitive Impairment, which is an ever-increasing danger as we age. Study of this problem has shown that taxing the mind on a daily basis does help a bit in keeping this MCI at bay. Regularly playing bridge or chess, reading a lot, writing letters, along with all the physical stuff from gardening to golf, offers a distinctly greater level of protection against this cognitive decline, as well as against senile dementia, Alzheimer's, and the rest. So, as the former British prime minister, Clement Attlee, said at the peak of his power, 'Just ignore the headlines and stick to crosswords.'

Various clinical studies at Stanford University and elsewhere have also produced data on how much the brain can be stimulated, and even Alzheimer's effects reduced, by certain other regular activities. And irregular, highly varied activities as well. At the top of the list, surprisingly, is the energetic dancing mentioned above, which is said to reduce the onset by (and don't ask how they worked these figures out so precisely) some seventy-six percent. This is followed by board games, which come in at seventy-four percent, then playing a musical instrument which gives a register of sixty-nine percent, but doing that daily crossword comes out on the list at a measly thirty-eight percent. Mind you, a friend saw an old lady taxing her mind in a similar way by trying to solve what she thought was a jigsaw puzzle. Unfortunately she was doing it with the contents of a cornflakes packet.

Not so surprising is the positive effect of listening to music of any style. Remembering the words and tunes of songs stimulates brain cells enormously, which is why, presumably, so many of those musicians and orchestral conductors live to such a ripe old age. One elderly relation soon came bustling back to life when prompted to sing a range of well-remembered old Scottish songs.

Alzheimer's afflicts about four hundred thousand people in the United Kingdom and over four and a half million in the United States. When President Reagan succumbed to it, his wife Nancy began to support the cause of embryonic stem cell research to help try to find ways of countering what she movingly called 'the long goodbye'. Having in the past been a strong backer of the pro-life lobby, and believing in the sanctity of the human embryo, her experience changed both her mind and that of many others. For as we age, by far the biggest of our worries is that we are going to go gaga as we do so. Many of us would rather die first. It's only natural because we see it happening all around us. Minds, memories and personalities get washed away. It's a tragic way to lose our friends and relations if we can no longer talk to them or they to us. We become particularly concerned if we've had parents who suffered from its debilitating effects. We remember the sadness of looking after them in their totally depend-ent state.

So we've got this crucial task of keeping our mental reach within our grasp. It's not just the less intelligent who get hit by mental misfortune. We've probably all come across some very clever people, including a few brilliant scientists, writers and academics, who have lost the plot years before they left this world. It's a safe bet that the same dangers apply to top bankers, cap-tains of industry, and even to those from the creative world of the arts. But if we are to believe what we are told by those who are working in the field of psycho-gerontology, age deterioration is still greatly slowed by a range of these brain taxing pursuits. While there are many conflicting arguments on this front, and many great minds have crumbled as they have aged, everyone seems to agree that if we sit and vegetate, our minds are much more likely to fall asleep.

If we can still express ourselves reasonably clearly, then we're probably still OK on the mental front. If we or others begin to notice that we speak with less clarity than we used to, it may be worth consulting the experts. There are lots of discreet little tests and exercises for incipient Alzheimer's available, which we or they can try out, that may indicate whether we are in tip top form or are maybe moving towards long-term memory loss. Some of these tests concentrate on questions about current affairs, such as asking us to name our member of parliament or senator, or the last three kings, queens, presidents or prime ministers of the country in which we live. We mustn't get too up-tight if we don't know the answers to such questions. It may be nothing whatsoever to do with our memories but more to do with our switching off on many aspects of contemporary life. There are similar short-term memory tests which include questions about what we had for supper last night, or what we watched on television yesterday, or whether we've taken our pills today. We'll all respond very differently on those fronts, no matter what our age. Many of us, through-out our lives, have never ever been able to remember such trivial details.

'I'm just wandering. I think of things, and then they go away for ever …' The novelist Iris Murdoch spoke of ideas going away for ever to describe her inabil-ity to write because of her incipient Alzheimer's. If we're seriously starting to worry about it we should go and consult a specialist. But don't get too hung up on minor incidents of forgetfulness. We all reach a time when we think our memories are going. 'Am I losing my marbles?' a friend asked the other day. He wasn't. He's always been notoriously forgetful.

Look back in time. How often in our youth did we forget many important facts, names and places? How often did we lose things of importance? A recent poll suggested that seventy-five percent of people only in their fifties admitted to frequently going into a room and then totally forgetting why they were there. So we've lost some item of value, have we? If so, there are a range of well-established routines. Where were we when we last remember having it? Going through a mental diary of where we've been since, and then retracing our steps is standard practice for all ages. Tidiness helps even the young in this regard. But there are things to beware of doing if we think we're really getting a bit absent minded. On no account must we try to prod our recall by putting things like credit cards and money 'where burglars won't find them'. If we do then as likely as not we won't find them later either.

As we look at our present partners across the break-fast table, after we've reminded them several times not to forget to take those pills, think back to Elvis who sang, 'I forgot to remember to forget her', or something like that. It's like the old man's even older joke, about tying our shoelaces in the morning, and asking ourselves what else we should remember to do while we're down there. Whatever else, there are lots of good ideas to help prod one's memory when we think our short-term type is starting to fade away. Notepads, diaries and reference books are useful tools for all ages. And if we seldom go shopping, don't worry if we don't know what things cost today. We can always remember the days when a loaf came to less than a few cents, or cost a shilling in old British money.

One favourite fridge magnet reads, 'I've not lost my mind; it's backed up on a disk somewhere.' If anyone starts complaining about us on that front, tell them that forgetfulness traditionally goes with brains and brilliance. Think of all those tales of absent-minded professors and Nobel prize-winners. Don't we remember from our youth a cartoon of one such professor dangling his fob watch in a saucepan of boiling water

DARLING — IT WASN'T YOU SAVING ARISTOCRATS FROM THE GUILLOTINE — IT WAS THE SCARLET PIMPERNEL AND IT'S FROM A BOOK BY BARONESS ORCZY...

and staring at an egg in the palm of his hand? Unreliable memory, along with all those wrinkles, inevitably walks hand in hand with reaching our prime. And talking of 'prime', do at least remember to keep repeating that we've yet to reach it.

As we age we can all get a bit confused in unfamiliar surroundings. It's like the long retired businessman who checked into a very modern hotel, and, after a while, rang down to Reception to say that he couldn't find his way out of his room. 'But, Sir,' the receptionist explained patiently, 'there are only three doors in your room aren't there?' 'Yes,' came the confused reply. 'So what's the problem, Sir?' 'Well one is into the fitted wardrobe … One is into the bathroom… And the third has a notice saying *Do not Disturb* on it.'

There are distinct rays of hope cropping up the whole time on the memory front. While there are no memory-related major prescription drugs on the market as yet, there are an increasing number of effective measures to prevent or postpone the onset of Alzheimer's before any lasting damage is done. There's always lots of talk about gene therapy and of new medicaments called 'smart-pills', or 'brain-boosters', which, in addition to the offerings of this book, may in future offer a 'Viagra for the Mind'. One type is codenamed

HT-0712. It reportedly can be used by students with poor memories when they are sitting exams as well as by the elderly. The drug apparently works on a memory gene within us, and so far it has been tested on mice and fruit-flies with apparently startling effects. So over the next ten years or so, we may be able to pop some pill, treating memory-loss like any other ailment, and remembering things just as well as any fruit-fly.

There are some important political side-issues that should concern us here. *The Washington Post* recently reported that, with four and a half million Alzheimer victims in the United States, medical and political experts are considering the dilemma as to whether to allow them to vote, if only to stop them becoming targets for political exploitation. But don't worry on that front too soon. We are not necessarily suffering from Alzheimer's if we can't decide which contemporary politician is worthy of our support.

In summary, why not let's argue that a failing memory in older age is largely to do with our brains getting filled up with far too many superfluous facts. It's like our computers: too many files lead to information overload. Something's got to give unless we keep pressing the mental 'save' and 'delete' buttons.

As we age, and we all do, our minds and bodies inevitably degenerate. We start worrying. Our overall fitness is collapsing. Our hinges are full of twinges. Then there's our mental health. Eleven pennies short of a shilling? Elevator not quite reaching the top floor any more? Confusion, repeating ourselves, mood swings, disorientation? Long before the doctors get to us on any of these fronts, we can still do a lot to stem the process. Healthier bodies have a proven, positive effect on our mental health as well. Fitness and mental agility for our age and as we age, are keys to a long bright future.

CHAPTER NINE

Bonfire of the Cardigans

'I'm saving that rocking chair for the day when I feel as old as I really am.'

– Dwight Eisenhower

The late Pope, John Paul II, when he was still a cardinal in his native Poland, was once taken to task by someone who pompously complained to him that 'Cardinals shouldn't ski.' His reply was simple: 'No. Cardinals shouldn't ski *badly*.' Now is the time to marshal all the simple little stereotypes and slaughter them one by one.

When it comes to our dress and behaviour, everyone is their own best mentor; not just of how we behave and what we wear, be it darned cardigans, crumpled jackets with the buttons in all the wrong button-holes, or badly stained trousers. What about the claret and coffee marks on our ties, our wrinkled, mottled complexions, unkempt hair in all the wrong places, especially mixed with snowdrifts of dandruff on our shoulders? Then there are the flagging, flaccid body parts, backed by a slovenly, stooping stature. Time has shaken us, stirred us, and in a bright light we can easily start looking as if we are on our way to oblivion. There are many things about this lifeline progress of ours that we can't do much about, like unsteady balance or worn out limbs, or minds that have become a little blunted. But with much of the above, we can do something to improve matters quite dramatically.

SENILE STEREOTYPING

The other day, an elderly man, recently confined to

a wheelchair, made a supreme effort to pull himself to his feet. Then, steadying himself with one hand on a side table, he began, because the wheels had got stuck, beating the wheelchair with his stick for all he was worth. 'Temper, temper,' needled his wife with a resigned sigh, which had the result of refuelling his wrath. Had we observers not been there, he might have turned the stick on her. Yet observers of this little scene, which ended, thankfully, with everyone laughing together, tended to sympathize. It was just the same as television viewers laughed and sympathized with John Cleese, when he beat his humble Mini car with the branch of a tree, when it died on him in one much-loved episode of *Fawlty Towers*. To keep spicing things up, age needs sage and thyme, but not too much basil …

Hot flushes? Menopausal mood swings? Do we kick the table, or the cat, in frustration? Have we started making lists of things on old envelopes in order not to forget? Do we scrabble to find the right word, and start calling everyone 'dear', because we can't remember their names? All these stereotypes abound. We are often seen, even by medical and other professionals, not, as we should be, as people of intelligent tranquillity, but as rigid, self-absorbed hypochondriacs. We may sit around bemoaning the iniquities of the present, but we are not all as we are perceived to be. One recent bit of research compared *The Trailblazer Generation* to college students. On that front, the latter were universally found to be far more neurotic, negative, lacking in self confidence, dissatisfied with life, unhygienic (!) and socially inept. The difference was that when the young were angry, intolerant, depressed (which is much more common with young people), or withdrawn, they were seen to be suitable for counselling or psychotherapy. We were not.

Another interestingly positive study, again out of Canada, tasked a group of young students, and a second group that were all in their seventies or older, to telephone the researcher at a set time over a period of weeks. The older age group were expected to do badly memory wise. In fact they did much better. You've already guessed why. Yes, they wrote themselves reminders and were almost perfect in their responses. There have been numerous other studies, including learning a language from scratch, where older age groups did just as well as younger ones, not least because they concentrated more and gave more time to it.

MIRROR IMAGE

Mother Nature gave us our face in youth. It's largely been up to us how it looks in old age. In youth it was like a grape, and when old like a raisin, but that can cover something just as tasty. A raisin is, after all, just a mature grape, and a man's wrinkles can be seen as emblems of a long and successful life. Women may have more of a problem on that front. There is a clever Spanish saying that hair (with added colour) can deceive, but wrinkles, the crow's feet around the eyes, reveal. Or we can redefine them as laughter lines. We may also notice that our skin takes longer to heal these days. Apart from all those liver spots, it can get a bit dry, so we need to invest in a good face cream. Come to think of it, if those liver marks weathered up a bit more and then linked together we'd end up having quite a tan.

With the march of time, all such facial characteristics define us, even though we may feel that underneath that outer disguise, we are still the same person we were in our youth. Yes, wrinkles should be considered lines of distinction, though few recognize this, and of all the great artists, perhaps only Rembrandt drew and painted ageing faces and bodies that also show intelligence and dignity. Our faces become our biographies, and when people start complimenting us on how we look, we need to watch that we keep our dignity. A famous beautician made the remark that time was not on her patients' side, but she was. At the age of fifty, everyone has the face they deserve. Our faces can be an index of our age, and wrinkles are the price or penalty we pay for not dying young.

We wanted to live long, we have lived long, but we don't need to look prematurely old in the process. We have to relearn to live appropriately. There are dozens of other things apart from the lines on our faces, that, taken together, suggest decrepitude. They should be firmly banished. What we need to do right now is to go and get a pencil and a piece of paper and write down a list of all the silly signs of ageing we have seen or experienced in others, things that we ourselves can easily abolish once and for all. Let's look hard at the most significant of them.

Youthful allure has a sell-by date. The actress Helen Mirren is, apparently, Britain's top naturist: she's well over sixty and claims that she still strips off all the time. Most of us, as we age, look at our bodies not so much with despair as with resignation. Yes, old bodies like old faces can come as a hell of a shock. One morning they're there, staring at us out of the mirror. Who is that old geezer? Is it me, or is it my grandfather? We mustn't let our body shapes get us down. They may have crumbled, but life is still for living.

As we grow ever older, our current bodies inevitably become more acceptable to us. As with our faces, maybe it takes longer in the mornings to make ourselves look presentable, but it's always worth the effort. We have to keep changing how we present ourselves. We no longer adopt the masquerade of youth nor need to ask ourselves whether we look our age. The key rule now is not to slop into bad habits over cleanliness, shoes, socks, or underwear that's long past its disposal date. Or toothbrushes. Maybe manufactures should put a 'Best by …' date on all things like that, since it's important to harness the bag-lady clutter that can become such a burden in old age. Don't get into the habit of keeping food that is past its sell-by date in the fridge. Some old people have things in there that are as almost as old as they are.

It's a phrase to keep repeating: we are what we appear to be to friends and outsiders alike. Perception is reality in all of life. A retired British army general was walking rapidly through Victoria Station in London one morning, when he spotted a beggar sitting on the ground with a hat in front of him, and a sign round his neck which read, 'Wounded Falklands War Veteran. Please give generously.' The General paused in his tracks, reached into his pocket, and threw a few coins into the man's hat. As he went on his way, he heard the Argentinean call after him, '¡Muchas gracias, señor!' That little story proves the point: image is what it's all about.

DRESS SENSE

Never let us hear ourselves say, 'This jacket will see me out.' Go and buy something new today. And keep on buying things even though you know they'll never wear out. Watch out if the end of our tie doesn't seem to reach the top of our trousers any more, and do something about it. If our weight has changed for the worse, that can easily mean that the clothes we used to wear, and still do, may make us look more upholstered than dressed. Remember the old joke about Michael Foot, the then leader of the British Labour Party, turning up at a Remembrance Day service at the Cenotaph, wearing an old suit and a donkey jacket, long white hair blowing in the wind? It went, 'How the hell did he ever escape Bonfire Night?'

'The Three Ages of Man: youth, age, and … You're looking wonderful …'
– Anon.

All of which means asking ourselves what clothes we should consider 'age appropriate'. We have to look the part we want to play. We must act our age. No mutton dressed as lamb. No ageing dandies. Watch that we keep the reality and the image close together. Dress like a clown or a down and out, or look like a Salvation Army reject, and that's what we'll be taken for. The difference between that clown and someone trying to act young is that the clown knows he's wearing ridiculous clothes. If people come to the wrong conclusions about us it's our own fault. Sitting around all day in a patched pullover, unshaven, hair uncut and unkempt, threadbare tartan slippers on a worn out rug, dirty fingernails, a stained mug of tea beside us, muttering vile imprecations at friends, relations, or the world at large, will bring, not rewards, but more misery for everyone.

Whatever age we are, fashion writers seem to suggest that we are what we wear. No longer should we be trying-to-be-trendy thirty or forty-year olds, pretending to be young. OK, they can mock our cardigans, but comfort starts to come first. Not having to climb into a suit and tie every morning becomes most agreeable. But better make sure both socks are the same colour. Remember too that fashion changes but style remains. Cords, jerseys, easy shoes, in modestly modern colours, should make office-bound men and women in suits, clutching their briefcases, laptops, and palm pilots, feel jealous, rather than disparaging of our easy style. After all, so many of their contemporaries go for comfort too, of the *Big Issue*, charity shop, variety.

There is one really *big issue* to be faced here. Should people over fifty (or do we mean fifty-five, sixty, or sixty-five, or seventy?) wear jeans? Why not? What about t-shirts, very long hair, dyeing the latter, or wearing body jewellery? We all know some aged Lotharios who do, and probably have done so since their days of sixties hippydom. They've never grown out of it. The answer is that it all depends on the shape of the person concerned, as well as their skin texture, suntan, etc. Not that there's any harm at all, indeed quite the reverse, in older generations being fashionable, though mutton dressed as lamb is always best avoided. The problem is knowing when that mutton is mutton. Oh, and if we have problems of a certain kind, don't wear light trousers that show stains.

Those who, fashion wise, refuse to accept the passing of the years, by packing or squeezing themselves into young fashion that even their sons and daughters would run a mile from, court ridicule. Yes, if we are like some male version of Zandra Rhodes or Vivienne Westwood, and go around attired like seventies punks (when we all dressed like demented Barbie dolls, so nothing today should, let's admit it, be considered weird), we may get away with it. Or we may think we do, while the rest of us smile wearily into our claret glasses from behind our more conventional exteriors. Other critics of our fashion sense, like crocodiles circling a canoe, will be much harsher.

Yes, there's one universal rule, unless we deliberately set out to wear purple, with a red hat which doesn't go, like Jenny Joseph promised in her famous poem. There are huge dangers in trying to dress as if we're still teenagers, with the peculiar business of having designer labels on the outside of everything. We have long been tempted to match Jenny, with a similar poem about ageing men, in jeans, leathers, tattoos, and too many dangly gold chains. It would not be wise, for instance, for a woman of a certain age, unless they were especially trim, to muster up the bravery needed to wear a bikini in public. A colleague remembers being hugely shocked some years ago by one of the most famous and ageing actresses of the day, a dame well into her sixties, going décolletée at a black tie dinner. Bits of her fleshy back hung over the chair she was sitting on. She would not have dressed like that if she could have seen herself from his vantage point. She should have followed the advice of the ubiquitous Oscar Wilde, who wrote that too much rouge and not quite enough clothes are always signs of despair in a woman.

TOO YOUNG TO BE OLD

'It matters not how a man dies, but how he lives.'
– Samuel Johnson

Toothless, grumpy, dishevelled, with a kind word for no one, turns a once charming friend and confidant into a latter day Scrooge, whom everyone will turn against or avoid. It's something that comes to both sexes. Women of a certain age will also harvest similar bouts of alienation if they succumb to crotchety ill-temper. Deep down inside we may feel we remain kind, caring and friendly, but we are how we are seen and heard, not what we really are or could be. The elderly have much to keep quiet about, and one advantage of that is that if we keep silent we won't be asked to repeat ourselves.

A hundred-year-old man had always eaten, smoked and drunk heavily. 'How did you manage to reach this great age?' he was asked. 'I know a man who did exactly the same, but he died in his late seventies,' came the follow-up. 'Ah,' chided the centenarian gently, 'he just didn't keep it up long enough.' To see ourselves as others see us comes with the rations of life. No one can change their image overnight. Remember Neil Kinnock? He started out as Leader of the British Labour Party, dressed in cheap lightweight suits, and then danced around in the waves at one seaside conference. Like his suits he was *seen* as being lightweight. Then his image-makers and spin-doctors got to work. Suddenly we had him on television, dressed in dark and sober pinstripes with a wall full of leather-bound books as a backdrop. The TV cameramen were instructed to film him from below to add to his gravitas. But it was all too late. That early image stuck. None of us can just press a button and change the frontage we have any more than we can change our reputations. And

'Age does not make us childish, but merely young at heart.'

– Goethe

if either starts sinking, it's a helluva climb back to the top.

Another man was recently accused to his face of having moved into his second childhood. What is it about that expression that infuriates? It conjures up an image of incontinence, dribbling, being spoon-fed, and having the mind of a one-year-old. Well that also happens, sadly. We know all that, but most of us can manage to avoid its worst aspects. Physical and mental decay is no laughing matter. Often the victim does not appear to notice, but, in the experience of professionals, they often do just that in the silence of the night. Uncared for by uncaring carers, with a brief insight, they recognize to their horror, the discomfort and embarrassment of such natural defects. It is those who look after them who take much of the strain. There are so many ways of countering many disabilities as the mind and body deteriorates, and the palliative care available these days has advanced hugely in recent years. The proper training of carers makes a massive difference too. We must never turn away. It may come our way.

It's largely about the lifestyles we live. If we're over sixty, we have seen a huge sexual revolution in our lifetime, and more social revolutions than any previous generations. Think of abortion law reform, the contraceptive pill, gay emancipation, female liberation. All that has happened during our lives, and our lifestyles have changed as well. Which leads easily back to what we, in our youth, thought of the crinkling aged and how they looked. We absolutely must not emulate them. We must not joke about the little problems that come along. Remember that sign outside the men's toilet in a hospital reception area which read 'Wet Floor. This is not an instruction!'?

We all know, even if we don't ever admit it, the problems of being caught short, or of minor incontinence. It happens from the baby's bedwetting stage, throughout our lives, given the right, or wrong, circumstances. In the British Embassy in Romania in the early seventies, the then UK prime minister, Harold Wilson, came out on an official visit to meet the deeply unpleasant President Ceausescu. Before the state banquet on the first evening of the visit, the PM gave a young diplomat personal instructions to come in after the main course, and whisper in his ear that he was wanted urgently on the telephone. The diplomat stood bemused, waiting for a further explanation. 'Just do as I say,' Wilson said, so the young man obeyed. At his rank, he was too junior to be a guest, but he waited on duty outside the dining room, in any case, for he might just be needed in an emergency. At the allotted time, and with his ambassador staring hostilely at him for interrupting that great occasion, the diplomat entered the room and went up and whispered in Mr Wilson's ear. The prime minister nodded, and followed him from the room, then immediately disappeared into the gentlemen's toilet. As his every move was monitored by the Romanian secret police, the Securitate, he deceived no one. There are easier ways of doing things, but that was his habit. We all need such help sometimes. Remember the helpful road sign on the M1 Motorway that used to read 'Emergency WC – 50 Miles'.

One friend, queuing for a theatre ticket, was recently asked if he was senior citizen, and if he wanted a concessionary ticket. He replied indignantly that he was under age, but the guy behind the desk, trying to be funny, said, 'Well, looking at you, you could be,' and issued him with a cheap ticket in any event. He didn't argue. Others would have hit him.

Other old friends, for the four decades of their working lives, were men of the smart suit and tie brigade. One, however, being of creative bent, probably did not even possess a tie. On reflection, though, he probably did have one which he had woven himself, from wool picked from the hedgerows in the early sixties, and dyed in psychedelic colours, by some simple and disgusting process, based on blueberries and urine. Now, however, most retirees revel in not having to wear the suits of office every day, and willingly dress down as is the fashion. We're paid-up members of the Cardi Club. We only reluctantly put on a white shirt and a tie when going out and about to the occasional dinner or reception, when our hosts still remember our continuing existence. The artistic one, by contrast, has now found respectability in his sixties, and dresses extremely smartly, his once wayward beard trimmed to perfection, to make him look like King George V or the late Tsar of All the Russias. Why not follow his example? Why not totally change our habits? Wear a cloak and a broad-brimmed hat. Grow a beard. It turns heads. It really does attract the ladies in particular. So the message is: whatever our past practices, don't let current standards slip. Comfort is in, but make it really stylish, with no patched pullovers, reading glasses on a string, which some of us have always had, and trousers with the creases running in a myriad wrong directions.

BITES AND PIECES

Time, they say, is a great healer, but it's no beautician. Do something immediately when we suddenly find a strange gap where a much loved filling has fallen out. Say no to yellow teeth. Having them colour coordinated with fading hair isn't much of a turn on. Getting back a big white smile is not so costly these days, and it will do a lot for our self-esteem. If they are still ours, our teeth that is, and if we and they continue to sleep together. Longer they may get as our gums retreat, but nowadays they don't need to be stained by a lifetime of cigarettes, strong coffee, and good red wine. A bit of bleaching won't dent our pensions too much, and dazzling white choppers staring at us out of the mirror of a morning does great things for body morale, even if the morals our body would like to experiment with are a bit beyond us these days. But watch out: it can cause gales of laughter if we suddenly appear complete with a set of gleaming, film-star implants, which can cost thousands and may still not last us out.

And as our eyesight goes, here's a little hint, based on studying large number of members of *The Trailblazer Generation*. We can all sprout a lot of extraneous facial and other hair. So go out and buy a really good mirror, with an excellent light on it, so that shaving really is shaving. As the Regimental Sergeant Major yelled at us when we did National Service, 'Stand closer to the razor next time!' We must avoid leaving large swathes of our neck and jowls looking like a cornfield harvested by the local village idiot. And watch those bushy out-crops of nasal and ear hair. Then there is our once full head of hair, or what we have left of it. It needs daily attention too. It can easily get so bad that it recalls the one great invention the French developed for curing dandruff … the guillotine.

MANNERS MAKETH MAN

In our youth we ran into difficulties. In old age, difficulties run into us. We must never try to emulate the young in matters of manners and behaviour. They have some modern habits we need not follow. For example, the following is again culled from groups of *Trailblazers*:

1 Keep on writing polite thank-you notes for dinners or parties.
2 Keep our elbows off the table, and don't speak with our mouths full.
3 Don't eat in the street.
4 Wear a suit and a tie at first nights at theatres and operas. OK, they are of no practical use, but they're good for our self-image.
5 Don't wear trainers or brown shoes with dark business suits.
6 Don't wear bleached, deliberately torn jeans.
7 Men: forget the body jewellery. Remember how we always despised those gold chains and gold bracelets over hairy chests.
8 If over fifty or fat, never wear baseball caps or t-shirts. Wear something loose.
9 Watch out if we find ourselves writing angry letters to newspapers that never ever get published. Ditto to local authorities, our MP or senator, the current

prime minister or president. Pay particular heed if we find ourselves writing in green or red ink, and underlining lots of words lots of times.

10 Don't buy a huge gas-guzzling 4x4 unless we live in the depths of the country. We don't need it. But if we want to buy a dashing open topped sports car, why not?

CLUTTERBUSTING

'Don't worry. You'll survive. No one dies in the middle of act Five.'

– Ibsen, Peer Gynt

We all need plenty of mental and physical body space. As we grow older we have to get rid of material things surplus to our present requirements. They are no longer just possessions, they become encumbrances. Possessions start possessing us. Eliminate … eliminate … Bring on the clutter-busters! As we grow older, we tend to hoard. Why? We're not going to need all those plastic bags, chipped mugs, stained ties, broken shoes, and worn-out shirts. The rule is SIMPLIFY. Cut the dross. Put the house in order and not just for the benefit of our successors. Clothes, old photographs (keep the best), very personal letters, files, meaningless knick-knacks, broken furniture: all these things should be binned since it will give us a clearer picture of where we are at now; and where we want to be. An absolute must is to throw the rubbish bags out straight away, or we'll find ourselves rummaging through them the next morning and removing most of the items. Let lots of new things into our lives. Go out and buy that new shirt. Or two, even if we know they are going to outlast us. It won't be us who has to send them to the charity shop.

Then there's the car. Do we need two any more? Or one? It's an unnecessary expense if we're travelling abroad a lot, and don't use it very much, except for the weekly trip to the supermarket. With licence fees, parking passes, insurance premiums, repairs, and a whopping annual depreciation, it costs us several thousands a year. We can take a hell of a lot of cabs and public transport before we even begin to match the road tax. At the very least we could trade in our old Ford or Volvo for something vintage, or that open topped something to bring back the wind in what's left of our hair. Vroom, vroom!

We know a lady who said that she left her husband to deal with the major decisions and problems of life, like world poverty, global warming, the fighting in Iraq and Afghanistan, and the problems of international terrorism. She meanwhile dealt with all the little issues: buying a house in Spain, planning another world cruise, and what new piece of jewellery she was going to get for Christmas. What other decisions do we need to take? Well, we may decide not to go on driving in the dark, then move on to selling off the car, then the lawnmower. We agree to employ more domestic help, and try, otherwise, to simplify our lives. We find more aches and pains creep up on us and we find it more and more difficult to reach our feet. The medicine chest is overflowing with past their sell-by date pills. It gets worse when we find we are wearing a pair of shoes, one of which is brown and one black, and that there's another identical pair at the back of the wardrobe.

To summarize, perception becomes reality in any walk of life. Clothes, hair, skin, deportment, attitudes, and the tendency to harvest clutter; letting our habits slip into decrepitude is the fastest possible way of making us feel and appear older, both to ourselves and to others. Keep a constant watch out for all those unnecessary signs of our own behaviour and rectify them at once.

CHAPTER TEN

Topical Tactical Tips

'... The sixth age shifts
Into the lean and slipper'd pantaloon,
With spectacles on nose and pouch on side,
His youthful hose well sav'd a world too wide
For his shrunk shank; and his big manly voice,
Turning again towards childish treble, pipes
And whistles in his sound.'

— Shakespeare, As You Like It

This chapter makes no apologies for containing some highly practical, tactical content. Facts abound, but they are important ones, since it would be wrong *not* to touch on some of the boring little issues we're going to have to confront. Without them we won't have the peace of mind and the stable backup to tackle the upfront problems of *The Trailblazer Generation*. For example, home is where the hearth and heart are. But it used only to be the place we came bouncing or wearily back to after a long hard day at the office. Now it has become the one hundred percent central stamping ground quite possibly for the rest of our lives. Is this where we really want to be? For the rest of time? Do these four walls contain all that we want? Is our home sweet home too big, too small, too old-fashioned, too inconvenient, too much of a burden, too cold and draughty, too gloomy? Now is the time to face up to deciding about the physical ambience we want for the remainder of our regenerated lives.

Maybe a bit of outside help would come in useful here. These days counselling is largely seen as being for the young or the middle-aged. But *The Trailblazer Generation* could sometimes do with a bit of counselling too about how to live our lives effectively and happily from now on. We may need advice not just on financial planning matters, but on health and safety issues that will increasingly affect us. We need it before any problems arise. We need help to avoid ourselves becoming locked into unsuitable living conditions or unhappy relationships with others. Negative images die hard, and, contrary to widespread belief, older people can be helped to change their ways of thinking on all such matters.

IMPROVE OR MOVE?

The one big issue that creeps up on us is improve or move. Why, when, where, how? What we need to do right now, maybe with a bit of help, is to log in the key implications of moving home, both positive and negative, or bold or timid. And when it comes to housing, so much depends on the ready cash or disposable assets we have to cover all the options we'd like to choose from. In addition, along come the three 'Fs': family, friends, familiarity. No lectures are needed here beyond putting out a big warning sign: we must make any of these decisions *within our own time frame*. No way must we leave it too late, when it may be forced upon us by ill-health or other circumstances. And if we do move, make sure it's to a house that we've surveyed with great care and that's had all its faults put right.

Think of all the well-publicized excitements and dangers of 'retiring to the country', to an apartment in sunny Spain, or Florida, or merely downsizing into a smaller place just round the corner. We've doubtless already been alerted to the many problems of striking camp and pitching our tent anew in an area far from the family, the friends and the environment we've always known. On the other hand, why on earth live in a big old-fashioned house, when we could loosen up some free cash to use on doing something like enjoying ourselves? We've probably come across lots of people who argue strongly that moving at this key time of our lives presents a mega opportunity to do something sparklingly new. They are the unchallengeable advocates of relocating to the seaside or the countryside, and seeking adventure in such pastures new. They've done it, so, like missionaries, or those who offer guidance to newly released prisoners, they urge us to go off and discover a new identity for ourselves, with lots of new friends thrown into the bargain. We can, they comfort us, find exciting clubs and groups who will welcome us into our new environment. On the back of this happy scenario, they continue, making such a break with the past provides unlimited stimulation to brains and bodies that otherwise will addle or fade away. The bleak alternative of staying put where we've always lived, dozing away each long afternoon and walking the dog along the same old paths, is a dead in the year option.

Other people take a totally contrary view: keep what you have, and, to use the contemporary jargon, outreach your future from there. If we like lists to help us make our minds up, there's one a mile long to ponder over when tossing a coin on whether to move or downsize. Here's a researched flavour of what it might contain.

- The likelihood that our present or future properties are too large and expensive to heat and maintain.
- Given that we are going to be spending much more time in our homes in future, are we still going to have enough room to do what we want?
- Patch into this equation the social, financial and physical costs of relocation, and whether our current furniture and possessions will fit in to any new home.
- Is where we are going within easy reach of shops and the local pub? Are there enough decent community and health services available?
- Remember the future! Is the splendid new property we're thinking of moving to, going to suit us, not just over the next few years, but also when and if we, or our partner, become infirm with age? Boring it may sound, but stairs and the number of floors can become a problem even for the ageing supermen among us.

- And then what if and when one of us dies? Would our distraught partner really like living there on their own, in terms of local amenities, friends and relations, safety, noise, and all the other factors mentioned above?
- One thing both the movers and the stay-put camps are agreed upon: before upping to the country, the seaside, or abroad, it's essential to case the area, by going and staying locally for a lot longer than a week or a brief holiday, to make sure it really is going to suit.

EVENTIDE HOMING

The majority of older people in most western countries actually stay firmly put in the homes they have always lived in. As they grow older, they get local social services to assess their needs, and, with the help of Meals on Wheels, home helps, and day care centres to back them up, they decide that they can exist pretty well on their own, thank you very much. Others choose, or are forced by infirmity, to move into residential or nursing care. That's where the boys of the old brigades have gone to live, and where the old soldiers who never die, have gone to fade away. There are lots of other such witticisms that have a similar ring to them, such as old professors merely losing their faculties, and moving into academic eventide homes, and journalists burying their last deadlines in the final newsrooms of life.

The image of the modern retirement home, creaking with the sound of rocking chairs and log-jammed with wheelchair traffic, is usually far from the truth. Most are extremely agreeable and well-run, giving their stimulated and lively residents a remarkable degree of independence when they want it, and like-minded company when they choose to mingle. However, some old people's homes can, sadly, with little help from uncaring descendents, become dreadful warehouses to store the elderly. If residents suffer from Alzheimer's, or are otherwise prone to distress, some of these places are known to use drugs as chemical straightjackets to control their behaviour. Move into them, and the dangers of the most active of us becoming rapidly institutionalized is always hovering around, quite apart from the vultures who own them gobbling up all our lifesavings. And do they take our pets as well? For very understandable reasons, many do not, so add that to our for or against list in deciding what to do.

Sheltered housing means a helpful style of living, though an old friend keeps referring to it as secure accommodation, which means something very different to those with experience of the criminal world. Retirement housing, accommodation that is specifically designed for older age groups, with certain common facilities such as a sitting room area, a laundry, and a resident manager, sounds good if we want to spend the rest of our lives exclusively with other elderly people. But check carefully, if either buying or renting, what the consequent service charges are. And, as always, think what might happen if our health deteriorated markedly over the years ahead. We're not going to try to compete here with all the detailed and constantly changing public and private care advice on all this; it's widely available from local authorities, and from organisations like the Abbeyfield Society, who manage nearly a thousand homes up and down the United Kingdom.

With eventide homing of whatever sort, crucial condition number one is the professionalism and pleasantness of the staff. One apparently tranquil and beautiful home that was recently visited, had an all-pervading and atrocious smell about it, the matron was a martinet, and the staff would have been better employed in a young offenders' boot camp. By contrast, the growth of retirement villages, and even towns, is an exciting prospect already much in evidence in the United States. In Europe we are tailing far behind, though in the Netherlands they are in process of building a *Senior City* in Zeeland. It will have neither schools nor discos nor tattoo shops, and motorcycles will be strictly banned. Like the idea?

GRANNY FLATTING

Grandpa or granny flats? Don't procrastinate. To repeat, if at all possible make such decisions within our own time-frame. Don't leave things until our senile dotage, when our offspring will have to make our minds up for us. Avoiding becoming a burden starts here. Watch out for that dependency culture. Parent-caring is a growth industry, and it needs a lot of careful thought and attention from both generations,

MOST IMPORTANT OF ALL, I WANT HIM TO ACQUIRE THE BEST OF ALL POSSIBLE TASTES... IT MIGHT BE HIM, IN THE END, WHO IS RESPONSIBLE FOR OUR OLD FOLK'S HOME...

just as caring for the care-giver is also crucial in similar sets of circumstances.

Of course if there is space enough for parents or offspring to build or alter their houses to incorporate a self-contained unit of sufficient personal style and space to raise it to the level of a Granny Flat (Grandpa Flats are rarer), then that can be great news. But a bag of experienced advice from all quarters calls for a totally separate entrance, bedroom, sitting room, bathroom and kitchen. Failing a separate front door, there's got to be an internal one that can be firmly closed by either party. Even in the closest of families, a degree of independence, hand in hand with inter-dependence, is crucial, to give both generations their own real body space.

Back to the choice of retiring abroad. Sunny Spain, Majorca, Tenerife, Florida, the Bahamas? Many parts of rural or seaside France, Italy, Turkey or Greece? They provide the locations for eventide homes for hundreds of thousands of *The Trailblazer Generation*. In some circumstances we can even have our old age pensions paid locally. But this is a step to take when we can still step back from the brink. Never sell up at home unless we are totally confident that it's the right final decision. Rent it out if you can. Selling up in Bradford or Chicago, then going off with a pocket full of cash to buy a bijou bit of paradise in Benidorm or the Florida Keys, can be fraught with many dangers. Living in perpetual sunshine may be great for the first few years, but many people want to return home in their later years, particularly if their partner dies, by which time they may not be able to afford to re-enter their local housing market. Many surveys have been carried out of people who have retired overseas, and way at the top of their other concerns are the standard of local health facilities, the doctors, the hospital care, that they might have expected to find. All that needs a major health-check too.

Consider the following. As we think of downsizing, moving abroad, or into a retirement or residential home, note that the cost of living in even a modest home can be up to as much as £100 ($180) a day. If, rather, we did what some people really do, and booked ourselves, long term and with a senior citizen discount, on a cruise ship, that can cost even less. On such cruise ships, which used to be known as God's waiting rooms, we are treated as passengers, not as inmates or patients. We get given superb service; we can have breakfast in bed every day of the week, as many meals as we want (most ships offer five or six eating opportunities a day), swimming pools, and gymnasiums at the end of a lift, free laundry facilities, non-stop travel, and in-ship entertainment. And we can meet lots of like-minded people as we see the world, living in agreeable climates. No worries about heating costs, dusting, doing the garden, changing bed linen, or getting the television fixed. We don't even need to buy our own shampoo, and if we die on board, a satisfying burial at sea, at nominal cost, is always a happy option. We're thinking hard about it …

TRAVELLER'S TALES

Even though we have, throughout our lives, taken a great number of key decisions, once we have retired for some time, it becomes increasingly common to find difficulty in making quite simple choices. Whether and how we should travel on holiday, can, for example, take on major significance. We used to commute regularly by car, train, or bus. We constantly flew on business trips and we got totally acclimatized to all the hassles of electronic tickets, checking in, security, and eating indigestible airline meals at all times of the day or night. De-acclimatizing, particularly since security and travel practices are constantly changing, can infuse panic in us in a remarkably short period of time. It's only a matter of a year since one acquaintance stopped travelling on a weekly basis between Scotland and London. Now, quite apart from the train or flight, there's all the fuss of him getting to the final destination at the other end. Even checking into a familiar hotel can suddenly become less smooth. And now *we're* paying. No more expense accounts; no more hotel and travel bills being sent straight to the office for payment.

SLIPS AND TRIPS

As we age and no matter how active and productive a life we of *The Trailblazer Generation* may be leading, at the top of any of our lists must come the crucially important matter of personal security and safety in all its aspects. As we become less physically alert, we worry more and more about our personal vulnerability: burglary, getting picked on or mugged in the street, or antagonizing some baseball-capped moron in a white van into some road rage incident. Too many domestic crimes and accidents involve the older generations. But there's no need to get too flustered as we age. We're far more likely to succumb to self-injury than to be burgled. There are far greater dangers in neglecting any necessary repairs and maintenance to our homes. Emergency plans and having easy access to telephone support from well-trusted artisans, delivers peace of mind. Having reliable neighbours' phone numbers handy is another must.

Real and perceived security, both practical and emotional, is rather like those safety instructions when we board an aircraft. Seatbelts? Yes, particularly if there is going to be turbulence. Oxygen masks? Yes, in case the cabin depressurizes. But life jackets? Friends in the airline business can't remember any accident in recent history when those inflatable flotation devices were used. So why do airlines still carry them, particularly when most passengers never listen to safety instructions in any case? The reason is that life's always about watching out for the unexpected. Something nasty might just happen and we have to be ready.

Making sure our home is our castle, with our house and contents insurance policies fully up to date, is essential. Most burglary is carried out by opportunists who see a window open or unlocked. Getting good alarms and extra door and window locks, security shutters or blinds, and a chain or peephole in the front door, so that we see what stranger may have turned up unexpectedly, is another must. Conceal those valuables, and, if we're to be away for a longish period, think of having time switches that automatically put lights and radios on, particularly at night. The police advise that a very visible burglar alarm is a big deterrent. External intruder lights that also come on automatically may sound expensive but they can be a great help, particularly in dark areas, paths, or alleys round the house, where thieves could work unseen.

Boring but important. Where are all those other clues to a house having been left unattended? Milk bottles or piles of post can always be looked after by someone we know and trust, particularly if there's a neighbourhood watch scheme in operation. If there isn't one, why not help set one up? Keys should never be left in obvious places, even though we think that it is the most convenient place to hide them, like under doormats or an adjacent plant pot. Spare keys are best not left just inside the front door since that just helps the burglar get away more easily, rather than climbing through the window he broke through in the first place. Marking property and kits for doing this are readily available. That's hugely helpful in recovering stolen property, though most of such swag is, sadly, seldom recovered by the police. At the top of the list of fanciable items are videos, stereo equipment, computers, and jewellery. Try photographing and dating the latter, since such items can't easily be marked, but place a ruler in the photograph to indicate the size, which can be a help in tracking the items down.

Get the various alarm systems up and running well in advance of needing them. We've probably always had burglar and smoke alarms, or we should have had. Now we may need to think of having a personal alarm too, in case of attack or accident. The elderly tend to bounce badly and if we fall we can so easily end up in hospital. British Government figures, for example, suggest that around seventeen thousand people a year are injured trying to put on their socks, tights, pants or trousers. It sounds comical but it's not a happy statistic. A recent NOP survey recently questioned a group of people, all of them over eighty-five. Three quarters of them said that serious fall-related injuries only happened to people older than themselves. In fact around half of over eighty-five-year-olds fall sometime each year, which, sadly, is one of the most common causes of accidental death. No apologies, therefore, for some other common-sense things to think about:

1 Making floors, and insides of baths and showers, non-slip.
2 Having brighter and better lighting, particularly on stairways.
3 Never go around switching off lights unless we have to. It doesn't save all that much money, particularly if we use long-life, low wattage bulbs.
4 Having extra hand rails on stairs. It isn't a sign of weakness.
5 Ditto bath supports, to help us in and out.
6 Watching we don't trip when hurrying to answer the phone. That's a very common cause of domestic accidents.

7 Taking care when we're carrying anything. One hand for ourselves and one for whatever we're holding.

8 Watching out for things like trailing clothes, worn or ill-fitting slippers or untied shoelaces – another major cause of accidents. They cause far more accidents than cars.

NEIGHBOURHOOD WATCH

Friends and neighbours can be hugely helpful and reassuring as watchdogs and guardians as we grow older. But they're growing older too. There are however numerous companionship services around which will find people to help and advise, perhaps even staying with one for a while to make life more agreeable. Government statistics show that a high percentage of burglaries are carried out by bogus callers arriving unannounced at the front door. They come waving false identity cards, pretending to want to read the electricity meter or collect for some charity or other. Or they claim they want to unblock our drains, mend our roof, double-glaze our windows, or re-tarmac the drive or front path (a favourite scam). They then deliver exorbitant bills. Watch out for other crooks who arrive pleading personal distress and asking for help. For the former, ask them to give you your customer or meter number first, before you let them in. Or tell them to make an appointment, and come back later. In the meantime, check them out with the utility company concerned. This is particularly good advice for older age groups, since the thieves will have staked out the houses round about, and will have identified whom they believe to be the most vulnerable local occupants.

Sadly, there are lots of other sharks and spongers lurking around ready to rip us off given half a chance. Always look for independent references. Shun cold-callers who, hopefully, are about to be banned in all European countries. Always take expert advice. Always get two or three quotes. Watch the smilers with the knives who tend to target the elderly because they're believed to be more gullible and vulnerable. Prove them wrong. The other big scam we have to watch out for are the 'antique dealers' who come along, usually with big white vans, and offer ready cash to the unwary for various bits and bobs of furniture and pictures, which they then take away with them. Fifty quid in used fivers for a rather battered old chest of drawers, a stained desk, or a nice little Victorian painting, which we hardly ever use or look at? It may sound attractive, but not when we realize later that our goods and chattels by now will be in a container bound for far away markets, before we, and our devastated descendants, realize what they were really worth. Newspaper stories of charming old houses being totally cleared out by bogus dealers only cover the tiniest fraction of scams like this. Ripping off the elderly is no better than burglary, so having an emergency helpline to call, if we feel bewildered or besieged, plus saying to the dealer that every single item is listed – with valuable items embellished with an invisible security code and all the alarms will go off if anything is moved, can send them running.

To repeat, it's a false economy not to install those burglar alarms, and also place signs on vulnerable windows, warning potential thieves that everything is alarmed. But check out the locksmiths and security companies that come to do the work. History is littered with crooked security firms whose owners and employees have learned their skills in the prisons of the land. Watch out too for those financial pirates who appear on television and elsewhere urging us to sell up our home and they'll give us money to live in luxury. That may well work for some, but think hard about the long-term repercussions and the effect on our descendants as well.

FACE LIFTING

We've all seen the sad signs of neglect in the houses of older people. Some are vaguely worrying; some are all too obvious. Such homes are often badly faded and in dire need of a serious face lift. 'I like things just the way they are, thank you very much,' is the spoken or unspoken, often deeply hurt response to the suggestion of change. It's hugely understandable but it's also due to our realization that, quite apart from the cost of a new kitchen or bathroom, fitting one would be a huge and tiring disruption. Equally, painting or hanging new wallpaper in the bedroom or living room would be pleasing, but, oh what a worry it would all be. And, back to the kitchen, please, no new cooking equipment whose up-to-the-moment, supersonic, airliner-type controls we would never master! Dealing with workmen and unfamiliar new kit, no matter what age we are, is a potential problem. So what do we do about it?

Back to some of those un-sexy basics. Let's presume that a kitchen or bathroom may need a bit of a face-lift every ten to fifteen years. That's not any sort of rule by the way. We've come across people of all ages who bankrupt themselves by installing new kit when the old was perfectly OK, just to keep up with modern fashions. Let's also presume that walls and paint-work, and particularly external work like windows, roofs, and gutters, could do with a touch up, or a major programme of redecoration and repair, every ten years. (Some of the greatest palaces and stately homes are touched up constantly, and consequently look exactly the same, generation after generation.)

The solution is to commission a professional survey to see whether a major refit or renewal, if affordable, is at all necessary. We should try to do this just before we stop earning, and while there's still a bit of an income stream, in case of unforeseen additional expenditure. So maybe in our mid sixties, redo the bathroom and update all its fittings, plus the kitchen, its dishwasher, cooker, and so on. Plus a total revamp of the central heating system, though take a lot of advice on that too. Then, around the age seventy-five to eighty, while we still have the will and energy to cope, have another real renewal or redecoration. Then, and only then, we may be allowed to say '*This will see me out.*'

To conclude this chapter, two splendidly true stories about external threats. One: an old lady, the mother of a close friend, went off on a bus to see her doctor. She had forgotten to get a specimen jar, so she used an old, carefully washed out, half-size whisky bottle instead. It was too large for her handbag, so it stuck out a bit, held in place by the zip. While she was paying for her ticket, and wasn't paying close attention, a young man pinched it, and jumped off the bus with it. He was laughing as he ran away … Another elderly lady takes her dog for a long walk through the park every day. She is fastidious. She tidies up after the dog, putting its residue into plastic bags, and putting them into an old handbag which she only uses for this purpose. She automatically disposes of the contents when she gets home. It is all she ever carries in that old handbag. She is briefly upset when a young yob on a bicycle rides past, grabbing the handbag, and making off with it. Later she laughs with friends when she imagines what follows.

No apologies whatsoever for this chapter's practical tips. Yes, it has been very much a matter-of-fact check list of dos and don'ts, in relation to downsizing, and keeping hold of or losing one's familiar domicile. On the housing front, from moving to maintenance, and everything to do with our own personal security, some of the check-lists set out above are worth looking at again and again. Or write your own. Without such peace of mind, all our *Freedom Year* strategies will fail.

CHAPTER ELEVEN

Getting On with Getting On

'Last scene of all,
That ends this strange eventful history,
Is second childishness, and mere oblivion,
Sans teeth, sans eyes, sans taste, sans everything.'
                           – Shakespeare, As You Like It

They say that old age is when you are ready and willing to give up your seat to a lady, but can't manage. By the way, if we really want peace and quiet on a bus or a train, try smiling and nodding at anyone who comes near us. It works. Old age is also having a choice of two temptations and choosing the one that gets us home earlier. Ditto being home on Saturday evening and, when the phone rings, we hope it isn't for us. But no man is an island. Grow old along with me. The best is yet to be. We know our John Donne and our Robert Browning, but we don't all know that Donne also wrote:

'No spring, nor summer beauty has such grace
As I have seen in one autumnal face.'

As they say, beauty is only a light switch away. Autumnal face … Nice term! We autumnal generations have a huge talent for grace. We need to use it, harbour it, display it. Maybe the occasional one of us can live life on our own, but most of us need relationships – family and friends – to keep the spirits alive and in good working order. They are good people to listen to, but even better to amuse. We have to aspire to be at ease with all ages. To feel out of place except with people of our own ages can be hugely destructive. Breaking the age–youth language barrier is another imperative.

DIALOGUE OF THE DEAF?

Many of us feel that communicating with the young is a difficult if not impossible task. So many of them, even if they're well educated, seem to be of the four-letter-word school of talking; and writing, probably with a spray can on a graffiti covered wall. When we watch them reading, we know they're doing so because their lips move. Mark you, there are a lot of older people who can't get a message across except with that unspoken form of communication … a smile, a scowl or a wink. In any event we have to remember that it isn't the whistle that pulls the train. Actions speak louder.

The famous American commentator, Garrison Keillor, is said to have once remarked that George W Bush's lips are where the English language comes to die. We may have an important message to put to the young, but is it understood? Speaking is not necessarily understanding. It's sometime a dialogue of the deaf. The same thing can happen with husbands, wives, partners or other close relations. We hear ourselves say, or are briskly told, 'You never listen,' or 'Talking to you is like talking to a brick wall,' or 'I've told you a thousand times,' or 'Are you deaf or something?' It's like the story of the man driving along a narrow country lane in an open-topped car. As he approaches a bend, coming the other way is another open-topped sports car, with a young woman driving. She more or less forces him off the road into the gutter. As she passes, she yells 'Pig' at him. He turns in his seat and yells something unprintable back at her. Then he pulls his car out of the ditch, drives round the bend, and hits the pig. We should prefer much more direct communication like the motorcyclist who, on the back of his black leather jacket, had painted the blunt words, 'If you read this, the wife's fallen off.' Children laugh at those jokes even when *The Trailblazer Generation* tells them, and that doesn't happen all that often.

What makes other people listen to us? What makes us reach for the off button in life? Dress, body language and paralanguage, the tenor and tone and enthusiasm of how we speak, are all critical. It's not so much what we say to our young, up to, say, the age of forty, but how we say it: the timing and circumstances, the resonance, and so on. After all, most of them learned to speak between the ages of three and five, and since then, unless they've been sent to elocution classes, few of them have had much further training. They don't need to sound like the average professional football player with their guttural utterances to have problems with their trying to communicate, and with our trying to understand them.

If we, on our part, go around muttering and moaning, looking decrepit, and behaving in a cantankerous manner, we're probably not going to hold the attention of even our nearest and dearest for long. We'll start overhearing them talking about us and what they're going to have to do with us, or discussing which old folk's home would be able to tolerate our behaviour. What we need to develop, or regain, is the ring of confidence that we once had, looking good, sounding good, standing tall. It makes people pay attention to us particularly if we use intelligent sound-bites. We also need to watch that we don't keep repeating ourselves or gradually adopting those incomprehensible grunts as well.

BREAKING THE BARRIERS

'Crabbed age and youth cannot live together: Youth is full of pleasance, age is full of care.'
– Shakespeare, The Passionate Pilgrim

We don't need to agree with Shakespeare. Some people also say that youth is wasted on the young, but with a little bit of effort on both sides the ages can live quite happily together. There are lots of tricks we can play. Remember that centuries-old card: if you're nice to me, you may benefit in my will. Someone once said that money isn't everything, but it sure keeps the children in touch. And keeping in touch is a hugely important subject as we advance in years. By the way, when we talk of the 'young', we mean anyone significantly younger than we are. It includes children, grandchildren, and their ilk, but it can also mean people a mere decade younger than us. They all think they know everything, but they can be pretty ignorant about the problems of growing old. By the time they've learned what it's all about and what is really important in life, we won't be around and they will be old in turn. Which is why we can possibly get away with being dangerously opinionated about the forthcoming pensions crisis or global warming. We won't be here when they happen.

When we get older we think we know all the answers. The trouble is that no one asks us any questions any more. Learning to cope with generations that seem to be getting younger and younger all the time is one of the issues we all come to face. We need to seize all the opportunities that are offered to communicate with them while keeping what we've always had: the space to do our own thing. Watch that we don't become a burden to them unless we have to through infirmity or other circumstances.

No pandering to youth. As we said earlier, some young people think we are the pampered ones, free-living pensioners stealing the future from them through the heavy taxation they pay to keep us. When we hear that argument, just remember: what has posterity done for us either? Getting all these things into perspective is crucial, like the letter the teenage girl wrote to her parents from her boarding school.

'Dear Daddy and Mummy,

I'm sorry to have to write and tell you that I've met and fallen in love with the school gardener's illiterate assistant. We've been meeting illicitly behind the sports pavilion after classes ever since the beginning of term, and I'm afraid I'm now pregnant. Now, wait, Mummy and Daddy! None of the foregoing is true, but I've just failed my mock English and Maths exams, and I just wanted you to get that news into perspective.'

GRANDPARENTING

Older generations have always been scandalized by the unthinking young. We're shocked by their apparently uncaring attitudes as when a young husband was recently heard saying that he and his wife had decided to have a family soon, while their parents were still young enough to look after them. Grandparents often fall foul of their children who complain that they're always criticizing or interfering. They and their grandchildren often seem to have a common enemy on that front. Even when those children become middle-aged, we still watch over them with concern and for signs of their improvement. We do so because we've brought them up ourselves, so we're still responsible and think we know better.

We have far more time on their hands now to watch, praise or criticize their darling toddlers than their fraught parents have. We think we know what will work and what won't. But any 'helpful' remarks we make can cause ructions, and relationships can become delicate or prickly to say the least. Intergenerational friction is what so many mother-in-law jokes are based on. So watch any remark like 'In my day …' or 'When you were young, I …' And don't try to buy affection by showering the third generation with sweets or toys without clearing it with their parents first.

We know some people who think that, except for special occasions, families are best avoided or ignored. The BBC, in a recent survey, found that a third of grandparents complained that they were too often taken for granted as a free babysitting service. Some generous British politicians subsequently announced a scheme to fast-track grandparents into becoming paid, registered, childminders … for their own grandchildren. We suppose that if that happens they'll get round to calling us granny-nannies. A wonderful new career opportunity, or… By contrast, a lot of grandparents are having far too good a time nowadays, travelling the world and so on, to want to go through parenting all over again, even if they were paid.

All in all it's better to be cautious about the degree of contact we have, a skill we should have learned from the experience of dealing with our own parents. We can teach but also learn what youth is thinking about and it's equally important to offer support without being overwhelming. And that means identifying that delicate balance between being there when needed and being intrusive. It works both ways, of course.

FRIENDLY FACES

We do all need to hold on to our remaining friends and relatives, especially if a lot of them have started shuffling off this mortal coil. It's all too easy to let long term relationships founder or disappear by arguing that 'I can't be bothered any more', 'I'm too tired', or 'parties are just for the young'. A great example is a next door neighbour, now well into his eighties, who has recently found a totally new lease of life, partying with the best and throwing parties of his own. And why not?

We could be overwhelmed by the choice of men's clubs, women's clubs, senior citizens' clubs, arts and painting clubs (if we enrol in a life drawing class, we never know what might happen), gardening clubs, film clubs, travel clubs, and so on. We may worry that finance is going to be a bit of a problem, but a lot of these activities either come free, or are not necessarily very expensive. This is especially true given the delightful for once, politically correct, 'let's discriminate against the young', culture. We can pick up a lot of greatly discounted travel tickets these days, as well as subsidized entrance to museums, cinemas, and theatres. Go for it. Go clubbing, and dress up to go. There's nothing like companionship to keep our spirits alive and kicking.

Which leads on to the controversial subject of reunions: school, college, regimental, etc. Some love 'em, some hate 'em. Ah, the stories that can be told. 'I wonder what's happened to old ...' Chimps share ninety-eight percent of their DNA with humans. So what? We of shared pasts, what do we actually have in common today? We spent a hundred percent of our time with some people at school or university over a year or so, welded together in those, our formative years. Let's have a look at what happens when we go to these events to see if the past will repeat itself. Will we still find him stimulating, and her attractive?

A friend hadn't been back to his old school for nearly fifty years. All those elderly strangers! He looked round and tried to see himself as those others saw him. He probably failed as much as they did. Where was the little boy inside that decaying lump? Where was that charming, bright girl with the sparkling eyes? He intended to try his best. He looked around him once more, smiling nervously. Why nervous after all that time? One or two small groups were talking together. Would someone greet him and pick him out with the nickname he once had? Would he recognize that smile, those eyes, that voice, the hair? No, not the hair. Nor the complexion, nor the body shape. Could they really all be of his age group, give or take a year? That couldn't possibly be true. Most of them looked so much older than him. In fact he discovered later that one or two old fogies were actually two forms below him. They'd all come bearing folders of photographs of school

plays, of Christmas pantomimes, of sports teams, of class groups. And in their back pockets and hand-bags they had photographs from today, of spouses, of houses, of children and of grandchildren, to be passed around and shown proudly to those who were not at all interested. OK, so my friend was biased. He knew of others who met regularly. First time round there was an initial awkwardness, but then they got on, chatter-ing away as if they'd just returned from their summer holidays.

We're here not because of the past but because of the present. Those whom we want to keep in touch with, we've kept in touch with. Our family is as boring to others as theirs is to us. On the other hand, what old acquaintances have done or have failed to do in life is something that might be quite interesting to discover. fifty years behind a desk at a bank? Decades buying clothes for some retail chain? Fascinating! But when a past friend has found real success, as Gore Vidal said, something inside us dies a little. No: we may not think that's necessarily true, but school or university could never ever have prepared us, those long years ago, for what actually happens in real life. By the way, how we laughed as students when a colleague's mother who had been at university in the 1920s, told on reunion that the biggest problem she was faced with each morning was which hat to wear to lectures.

WHERE THE HEART IS ...

'People ask me what I'd most appreciate getting on my eighty-seventh birthday. I'll tell you. It's a paternity suit.'

– George Burns

In our youth, the air was clean and sex was dirty. We learnt the hard way. But sexagenarians can still think about, if not act, the sex bit. Passions may be spent but we can still be passionate about other people. Yes, when our sex drive goes, it goes. But at sixty, seventy, or eighty, and if we're single, there are still a lot of dating games to play, with various organizations of lonely, ageing hearts waiting to help or adopt us. It can be fun, it can be exciting, and if it can still be … sexy, it can offer romance or even marriage. So the old can't find passion or fall in love? That outdated idea needs a total rethink as well.

Sex has always been a ladder to happiness or a trap-door to failure. They say that old men chase women, and when they catch up with them they can't remember why they bothered. We feel even older when we catch ourselves worrying about all those young girls with bare midriffs catching cold. By the time we've reached that stage, we don't need to give up our vices; our vices have given us up. Which can lead on to our complaining about other people's vices to which we no longer have the ability to subscribe. It's the same with temptation. It avoids us, though we'd still quite like to get close up to it. Sex or no sex, we have to keep nurturing our relationships. We reach the age we are and that's just fine. Our partner will have done so as well and physical desire may consequently have waned over time. The good news is that, with the waning of lust and sexual power, minds become calmer. It recalls that splendid Valentine's card which read 'To the world's best lover from the world's best actress'. Deep down we may be tempted to trade in our sixty-year-old for two thirties, or three twenties. 'Till dawn do us part' relationships have long gone. It's mostly imaginary these days, though, as Groucho and several others have said, 'Women keep running through my mind. They daren't walk.' Ah, all those fantasies …

We may recall the population census back in the sixties which had us all in stitches. The numbers were defined as being 'broken down by age and sex'. How we laughed. It's like the current American joke about ex-President Clinton who had sex between two bushes, or the old man who was asked what all the notches on his walking stick represented. Remember the pretty girl saying to the pensioner, 'Let's go upstairs and make love …' to which came the sad response, 'Sorry. I can't do both.' Physical desire between those over sixty can often appear odd and embarrassing to the young. For them it is difficult to understand. Let's leave it that way. They will, if they are lucky, discover it too in due course.

How about a quick fling? And we're not just talking about men. Oh no. There are quite a few predatory women who take passage on some cruise ships. They're out for all they can get, and who can blame them circling around the handsome young Filipino cabin stewards? Remember Richard Strauss's *Der Rosenkavalier*, where the ageing heroine falls in love with a lad in his late teens? It takes a lot of singing before she realizes it's far better to act her age and grow old more gracefully. By contrast, on one recent Caribbean cruise, one extremely well-turned out lady in her early eighties was proposed to, not just once, but twice, within the first week. She turned both suitors down.

A German philosopher once said that, given a degree of mutual attraction, if a man believed he might get away with it, most would opt for infidelity. Never forget that Pablo Picasso, Charlie Chaplin and Saul Bellow were still fathering offspring well into their eighties, just as some notoriously aged pop stars currently do, since they have the fame and money to keep on hooking. As for ladies of the golden age, remember that Shakespeare had Antony saying of Cleopatra that 'Age cannot wither her, nor custom stale her infinite variety …' That could be you, Madam! No problem about looking at attractive youth of whatever sex, since a bit of window shopping is perfectly OK. Even though we can't buy.

Groucho Marx used to say that a man is only as old as the woman he feels. If we feel that remark's a trifle coarse, the Bible has some pretty naughty sex stories in it as well. Remember the one about the ancient King David, lying ill and cold in his bed, so his aides went out and found a pretty young virgin called, somewhat eponomously, Abishag, to lie with him to warm him up, or something. It didn't do him much good, for though she 'Cherished the king, and ministered unto him', he still lay cold beside the poor girl.

TWENTY OR THIRTY YEARS AGO —
GIVEN THE SAME CIRCUMSTANCES,
YOU'D HAVE BEEN CHASING ME
ROUND THE ROOM BY NOW...

As an addendum to that, Clemenceau, the French statesman, at eighty (his age depends on where you read the story, and American books of quotations say that the incident refers to Oliver Wendell Holmes and others), was strolling along the Champs-Elysées one day when he spotted a very pretty girl, and remarked wistfully to his companion, 'Oh to be seventy again!' Another version of the same is of a man of eighty seeing the same pretty girl and saying that he wished he were twenty years older. Surely you mean younger, came his colleague's response. 'No, older, since if I were that age I wouldn't care a damn.'

MONEY MATTERS

> *'Cessation of work is not accompanied by a cessation of expenses.'*
> *– Cato the Elder*

Women like men with something tender about them, especially legal tender. OK it's a bad joke, but it makes a good point. After sex comes money. It always matters. This book does not attempt to compete, except in passing, with the many self-help books on practical aspects of money management, retirement pensions, and similar material issues which make our lives liveable. Contrary to the old saying that money doesn't buy happiness, it does if it is well managed. It's like those banks that leave their doors wide open, but chain their pens to the counter. It's the little things that matter. If we want to know about the details of post-retirement financial planning, books, usually published in herd instinct fashion by financial services companies, are out there, again to mix metaphors, in shoals.

Then there is insurance. A very few insurance companies these days have actually started taking into account not just a person's age, but their medical history. They point out the obvious, that someone over sixty-five can often be in far better health than some overweight person who is only thirty or forty years old. A lot of young people seem to die off years before they're buried, while some ninety-year-olds can have minds of thirty. So there's some good news out there. If we shop around, home and contents insurance can sometimes actually be cheaper because the more mature are rightly believed to be more security conscious; and car insurance can also work in our favour, at least until we reach seventy, when almost all insurers start charging us as if we were back in our irresponsible twenties once again.

Now let's talk briefly about the contemporary subject of SKI-ing. Which means 'spending the kids' inheritance'. One fridge magnet reads, 'Avenge yourself. Live long enough to be a problem to the kids.' With inheritance tax at the level it is in most western

countries, there's a lot of disincentive to pass money on to the next generation in any case. But there are no pockets in a shroud and, even if we are intending to be enormously generous to our descendants, we first have to make scrupulously sure we've kept enough money to live properly and enjoy ourselves for the rest of our lives. And we all need to become much better informed about pension matters. Leaving someone bereaved behind us, and sadly this happens all the time, who doesn't even know where the policies are kept, is a great sin.

The oft-repeated phrase is that two things are inevitable: death and taxes. Both hit us in curious ways. In New York, in the mid seventies, a case was pursued by the US Revenue Service against a cleric from one of that great city's churches. He had claimed tax relief on his subscriptions to both the *Wall Street Journal*, and *Playboy* magazine. His tax people allowed *Playboy*, but not the newspaper, since they declared that the latter 'lacked social relevance'.

WHERE THERE'S A WILL

Where there's a will, there are people out there who think they ought to be in it. The great piece of advice that was offered in the eighteenth and nineteenth centuries was not to let your doctor (and what about your lawyer?) know that he was a beneficiary in your will. A piece of very contemporary advice is that if your offspring are not behaving particularly well, next time they call round you can always leave some brochure about bequests to the RSPB or Guide Dogs lying around the house. There is masses of free information to be had on wills and estates and on hiring good independent legal and financial advisers. The only thing to add to all that is to ensure that they should, for obvious reasons, be at least a generation younger than us, so that they'll outlive us.

If we don't make a will our estate can be seized by the state. We don't want that to happen. We need to appoint executors who will make sure our wishes are carried out after death. We may have done a lot of that *SKI-ing* already but hopefully we'll not have been too mean. We have arranged enough to keep on enjoying life and even to employ someone to look after us when we are less capable. Because we may become unable to take rational decisions through a stroke or dementia, for example, it's also advisable to give a power of attorney to someone we can trust, so that they can take any such financial and property action for us.

Then to further secure our future, while fully fit and in control of our minds, we may want to create a so-called 'Living Will', also known as an 'Advance Directive', which gives us a degree of certainty as to how we are to be looked after both physically and medically in a less certain future. We must all react with horror at the thought of being kept indecently alive in body but not in mind. To obviate this, these can become our authorized wishes, via a legally binding document, about medical treatments and so on that we may wish to have, or have withheld, if we suffer from some terminal or incurable illness.

It is increasingly important, as we grow older, and there is a great deal of current evidence for this, to get help in simplifying our banking, investments and tax affairs. Unless it comes naturally to us, playing the stock market for a bit of fun now that we've got plenty of time to do so, has to be carefully monitored. Otherwise, having an easily managed portfolio for all our money matters is something to think hard about, since it can become an increasing worry and muddle for us as we age. We don't want any hassle on that front from now on.

The autumnal years for *The Trailblazer Generation* can prove the best of all. Relationships, from sexual to social, and in particular with the younger generations, become more and more important. How we communicate effectively with them remains ever more central to our lives. How we manage our money and our financial advisers underlies all the above as well.

CHAPTER TWELVE

Use It
or Lose It

'Old age has a great sense of calm and freedom: when the passions relax their hold, then we are freed from the grasp, not of one mad master only, but of many.'

– Plato

Growing old is no more than a bad habit, which a busy man has no time to form, wrote André Maurois. By now some of us will agree about that. As Yogi Berra and many others are said to have said, 'It ain't over till it's over.' The fat lady isn't even on stage yet, let alone preparing to sing. It's not our swansong, so let's keep going.

Despite all life's frailties we can still pick and choose what we want, and leave others to fuss about problems that shouldn't concern us. *The Trailblazer Generation* remains upright and on parade. No way must we follow the King Lear approach and be lured into a trap of handing over our power and possessions too soon. Remember how that poor monarch ended his days, blind, and bereft of almost all support from those to whom he bequeathed his kingdom. If we live to a fine old age, those around us are usually generous and praise us for our longevity, but on the way there unkindness can creep in. If senility starts to embrace us, some will rush around and help while others will mock or pillage, forgetting how we were in our prime. It is like those cruel obituaries where only the scandals or weaknesses of the subjects are recalled rather than the real contributions the individuals made in their lifetimes.

REACH FOR THE SKY

'It's not the men in my life, but the life in my men, that counts.'

– Mae West

If life had all been a bed of roses, how sickly that would have been. Squished up, gooey, rotting petals and leaves, and lots of nasty little pricks to go with it. In this, the Indian summer of our lives, we can drift happily into senescence or keep the fires burning in the furnace even though there appears to be a lot of ice on the roof top. The gods send nuts to those that have no teeth goes the tribal saying, but these days, we don't need molars to crack the opportunities that are still on offer. We need incisors. The main issue now is to keep seeking out these opportunities even though our mind and body tend to long for that comfortable armchair by the window. Why take part any more, we think, when we can safely dream of the past, and only look at the present by being voyeurs of other people's lives?

Frank Muir used to tell the story of having to have an operation somewhere around his nether parts. He was shown into a private room, and told to undress and put on one of those back to front, pre-operation frocks. Then the nurse shaved off his pubic hair, and left him alone for some time. When she returned, she knocked on the door and came in. 'Have you any questions, Mr. Muir?' she asked attentively. 'Yes, nurse,' he replied. 'Why did you bother to knock?' Thank God we live now. The medical and nursing professions have advanced hugely over the last fifty years. Hips, heart valves, pacemakers, kidney dialysis, eye operations, and cancer treatments: the list is never ending. Most pain can now be appeased, palliative care is much more advanced, and the hospice movement is a Great Success Story. Most of us nowadays can live without experiencing many of the hideous historical agonies and discomforts of past diseases. But we may still need help to cope.

But there are crucial things we have to watch out for, like rationing drugs for the elderly. The British National Institute for Health and Clinical Excellence (NICE) has on more than one occasion recently caused great alarm among older age groups by threatening to withdraw certain drugs used to delay the onset of dementia, on cost grounds. They have also been caught out arguing that discrimination on grounds of age in the provision of certain treatments is fully justified. Health economists are accused of using something called 'QUALY' (Quality Adjusted Life Years) to justify their view that older people who expect to live a quality life in mental and physical terms, should be allowed unlimited treatment and care. By contrast, the less fortunate among us should receive less costly palliative care. If that's not grotesque discrimination, what is? Age should be used for clinical convenience, not as a formula for diagnosis.

A little or a lot? Newspapers are crammed, particularly at weekends, with advertisements for lots of special equipment for the disabled or infirm that has become widely available over recent years. Powered bath seats, stair-lifts, Zimmer frames, walk-in baths, bath-hoists, motorized wheelchairs, emergency call-button systems, orthopaedic shoes, and glucosamine sulphate. And special bidets, which remind us of the occasion when Churchill was asked if he wanted one installed in the bathroom at Number Ten. Having just

had a spat with General de Gaulle, he was in no mood for things French. 'If someone wants one of those damn things, can't they just do a handstand in the shower?' he responded. Many of us have not got that far in this field beyond having their reading glasses hanging on a cord around their necks. Or occasionally wondering what equipment there is when they're having a little difficulty cutting their toenails. How we used to laugh at that hoary Channel Ferry joke: 'Harwich for the Continent; Frinton for the incontinent.' No longer. We may need to start thinking about what help we might need in future for shopping, cleaning, cooking, and, eventually, bathing. If we suddenly find ourselves trying to cook without lighting the gas first, it's time to act.

FOR WHOM THE BELL TOLLS

Every birth certificate has an expiry date. Amid all the longevity statistics one truth remains: the death rate is always one per person. Though some highly successful people die young and some unsuccessful people live to a fine old age, good social standing and success really does seem to ensure better

'I am ready to meet my Maker. Whether my Maker is ready for the ordeal of meeting me is another matter.'
– Winston Churchill

health, and the prospect of a longer life. Earning more than friends and colleagues and spending relatively more on our health, buys longer life. Yet, by contrast, it's a sad fact that we have all come across people who seem to be demonstrably old long before they reach their first half-century. Of one man it was said that he would be greatly improved by dying, and another was considered to be well past his sell-by date shortly after his thirtieth birthday. We come across people of exactly our own age who look and behave so very much older than we do. At least we think so. Let's try to belong to the club whose members remain sprightly and intellectually demanding. Don't bore. Don't let the grave yawn for us.

Facing our later decades we of course become a bit slower in our speech. We may find that others start finishing our sentences for us. Despite Shakespeare's gloomy warnings about derelict old age (and, in his century, he was an old man of fifty-two when he died), we mustn't ever find ourselves mentally joining the queue on the road that leads to the cemetery. We're not living just this side of the grave, though inevitably we are of the D-generation (pun intended). While we are now in our more physically fragile years, enjoyment still comes top of our list of objectives. We need to embrace more than just a touch of hedonism. Then, and only then, let us deal lightly with the inevitability of death.

There are no pills for every ill. For all the money spent on medical research, death is still the world's number one killer. By the time we're sixty, we've passed most of life's misfortunes except for this last one, and that's a risky business. One in three dies of one sort of affliction and one in ten of something else. But one out of one dies of something.

GRAVE MATTERS

There is a crash at the front door and the morning newspaper falls onto the floor. The elderly occupant of the house immediately comes and picks it up and takes it to his armchair by the fire. He ignores the front page and the sports pages,

'They say such nice things about people at their funerals that it makes me sad to realize that I'm going to miss mine by just a few days.'

– Garrison Keillor

the business section and the reviews. He sips his cup of coffee and turns instead, as he always does nowadays, to the death notices and obituaries. Why? To see whom he has outlived, to read how old they were when they died, and to study how the famous, the infamous, or the peculiarly interesting can be celebrated, ridiculed or condemned when they go. Written by professional obits writers from the newspaper's 'morgue', these pré-cised biographies can be flattering, boring, or a place to settle old scores. If the reader's name is not there yet (and we all remember Mark Twain's reaction to reading his own obituary, 'The report of my death was an exaggeration'), it still gives the reader some indication, some steer as to how long he has to go and whether and how he'll be noticed when he does.

If a teenager dies it is tragic. If a ninety-year-old passes away, he's had a 'good innings', living to such a 'ripe old age', and there are few regrets. The elderly around us seem, probably through our sad experience as veterans, to be better at coping with death and loss. We still prefer old age to the alternative of oblivion. But dying affects those left behind more than those who have gone. Even if we're not quite ready for eternity, it may be waiting for us just round the corner. We mustn't leave thinking about it until it's too late. If we don't start to prepare, it's our funeral, as they say. Whether we're rich or poor, famous or unknown, the end is universal. Death hits the headlines every day if we go looking for it. We increasingly miss people who've moved on. We spend time reading obituaries of people who have done so much in the distant past. We remember them in their prime. We occasionally read obituaries of people we believed had died decades ago. We wonder where all the other people we once read about have gone. We go to their funerals or memorial services, which Harold Macmillan called the cocktail parties of the geriatric set. We die as well.

Deeply loved ones move out of our lives the whole time. We like people whom we like to like us; we don't care a damn about the rest. We'll miss them if they go before us. Even the death of a much-loved family pet can add enormous amounts of grief. It's always easy to skirt around the subject of death. We would like to do so here, but it can't be avoided. We need muscle and determination in order to cope with it, the most important thing in life. Stoicism and serenity are needed. Death is the last frontier.

The shadows fall. Among the many things that any partner left behind is likely to worry about as death approaches, include the following:

1   Their immediate ability to cope with the death of their partner.
2   The consequences of this for their own health.
3   Their future financial position.
4   Their personal security, their house, their ability to run it and pay bills etc., particularly if their partner always undertook those tasks in the past.
5   The prospect of increased isolation and loneliness in the future. How will they be able to cope and socialize on their own?

The good news there is that, just maybe, it will be easier than they think; being single, that is. Many elderly men and women find their feet quite quickly, particularly once they're out of the shadow of a more prominent or powerful partner. Severe illness or bereavement can be traumatic, but there is a lot of research and anecdotal evidence that many people emerge stronger as a result of seeing the frailty of life in close up. Such events can act as wake-up calls, making us focus anew and plan afresh.

BEYOND THE PEARLY GATES

It is said that if the Archbishop of Canterbury declares that God exists, it's all in a day's work. If however he says that God does not exist, then something signifi-cant has been said. Few people are experts on such matters, and many others are definitely of the 'Man created God' school of thought. But on a recent five week cruise, a group of passengers, all of them well over sixty, were asked for their views on retirement, non-retirement, longevity, and how to grow old with grace or with mischief. A hefty number of them brought matters of spiritual

> *'Better to die on your feet than live on your knees.'*
> – *Che Guevara*

belief into the equation. Here are some of the phrases they came up with.

- Accept, spiritually, that death is an inevitable part of life, and prepare for it.
- Recognize that healing is not necessarily physical.
- Believe that prayers for healing can be successful, if you achieve peace of mind.
- Be compassionate. Give that you may receive.
- Be content with what you have. It will bring you peace.
- Love and affection breeds happiness and a longer life.
- Live holistically and in moderation.

Readers will have to make their own minds up on such wise and thoughtful words.

An anonymous saying is that 'Death is Nature's way of telling us to slow down.' A rather clever poster that appeared recently, advertised the benefits of nursing as a career. On it was a picture of an attractive young nurse holding a newborn baby in her arms. Underneath, the caption read, 'The first few minutes of life can be critical.' Underneath that again someone had written, 'And the last two minutes of life can be a bit dicey too.' That inevitably raises a most difficult question: we were all helped into this life, so why not get a bit more help at the departure gates if we are very ill, in terrible pain, and totally incapacitated? That is a very dangerous field in which to think of playing.

We are coming up to the final curtain. Irving Berlin wrote that the song is ending, but the melody lingers on. There's an old journalistic joke about a foreign correspondent sending a telegram from some war zone to his editor which read, 'It is difficult to exaggerate the gravity of the situation here, but I shall do my best.' On the subject of dying, while we all find at times that it's possible to bear with equanimity the misfortunes of others, we won't exaggerate, but will step quietly to one side. A friend remembers getting into a lift one morning in a very expensive hotel on Park Avenue, New York. It was filled with clouds of illegal cigar smoke. Through it he saw the ancient comedian, George Burns, whom he greeted with a polite 'Good Morning, Mr Burns.' That gentleman's instant, carefully crafted reply was, 'Good morning to you too, sir. You know that when you say good morning to me, it means I'm still alive. These days,' he added, 'putting my cigar in its holder is the biggest thrill I get.'

We see death all around us on a daily basis: wars, famine, disease, accidents, cancers, obituaries, cemeteries. Stalin wrote that one death is a tragedy while a million deaths is just a statistic. Some gloomy scientists are convinced that Homo sapiens may well be wiped out in its entirety some day. Many nasty viruses are so stupid that they kill off their hosts so quickly that they don't live long enough to infect those around them. Some new infection a hundred times more effective than AIDS, Ebola, or CJD, will come along. Experts believe that, like avian flu, they may get wiser and kill more. It may come to all that.

There is little point in harping on about harps, but we all, slightly nervously and constantly, joke about death. Is it to diminish its impact? In a world full of uncertainties, death is certain. It's the end result of living. We don't like to confront it but it's universal, from kings and prime ministers, to dustmen and down-and-outs. Finality is linked to tragedy for those left behind. It is a vital subject. Some believe that death is too dangerous a thing to laugh about since it always wins in the end and can be quite nasty in the process. But we are all equal when we get there. In the meantime, there's no harm in being 'in love with easeful death', and trying not to be too gloomy on the way.

Many professions are inextricably linked to death. Doctors and nurses are the first in line to give up on our lives, then come the funeral directors and the grave-diggers, and the writers of obituaries. The lawyers, auction houses, and estate agents pick up the pieces. Putting aside the ethical debate about things like euthanasia, dying with dignity is everyone's ambition. It is not longevity, but, once more, the quality of late life that matters. We have little wish to extend the life, even of a baby, if the reality of that life contains horrendous discomfort and pain. There can be nothing more devastating than the death of a spouse or close friend. In older age, relationships can become much warmer when there is less competition around, and that adds to the distress, like the old lady seen holding hands with her even older husband. Someone remarked that they were still so much in love. 'No,' came the sharp answer. 'If I don't hold his hand the whole time he'll wander off and get lost.' When asked if he would attend Marilyn Monroe's funeral, Arthur Miller's off-the-cuff remark was to ask why, since Monroe wouldn't be there.

The director of that memorable film *Death in Venice* was reputed to have been driving through a wet and miserable Huddersfield one evening, when he passed a cinema that was showing his film. At the door, dressed in a faded dinner jacket, was a dejected looking cinema manager. The director stopped the car, got out, and went up to the manager to shake his hand. 'So how is *Death in Venice* doing here in Huddersfield?' he asked. 'About as well as *Death in Huddersfield* would do in Venice,' came the grumpy reply. Death may be the last taboo, but, yes, we still manage to laugh at it, backed by the Bible's 'O death, where is thy sting? O grave, where is thy victory?' line. Just think of the number of jokes there are floating around about St Peter waiting for arrivals at these pearly gates. Or the one about the customer who goes into a stationer's. 'Do you sell *With Deepest Sympathy* cards?' he asks. 'Yes,' comes the answer. 'Then can I please exchange the *Get Well Soon* card I bought here yesterday?' Berliners in their final Christmas before the city's fall to the Russians in 1945 adopted much black humour on the subject. 'Be optimistic', they said. 'Learn English. Be practical: learn Russian. Be even more practical: give a coffin.' The 'till death us do part' is always a part of any life. 'I'm not afraid of dying,' says one of Woody Allen's characters, 'but I don't want to be around when it happens.'

Life runs only one way. There are no return tickets. Of course, the inevitable funerals are largely to appease the living who otherwise feel they've failed in their duty not to have arranged our appropriate rite of passage. We won't know about it so we'll be past worrying. Leave the handful of dust to others, but we do need to make sure we're prepared for it before it's too late. Hopefully we'll avoid the sort of reaction when some wag declared, 'I didn't attend his funeral, but I wrote a nice letter saying that I approved.' If death happens to a generation older than us, we see it as the end of an era. We are now on the front line.

There's a graveyard at Old Windsor, where, just inside the gates, stands a green, municipal rubbish bin. On the lid and on the side these words stand out: 'No hot ashes please!' This book does not set out to discuss graves and graveyards, nor for that matter crematoria, beyond suggesting that it is only fair to let our survivors know how we prefer to be sent on our way, while we still have all our marbles. The message continues to be about the living. In the long run, said John Maynard Keynes, we are all dead. But no, we are absolutely not going to be lured into writing about the hereafter. If people want to believe in a heaven above the bright blue sky, or a bubbling hell filled with demons poking at us with red hot tridents, then good luck to them. The old Norsemen believed in an icy hell, which maybe is marginally preferable. The trouble is that people who've died are not available to discuss their experiences. Benjamin Disraeli was, on his own deathbed, asked if he would like his long term admirer, Queen Victoria, to visit him. 'I think not,' he replied. 'She'll just give me a message to take to Albert.' Yet there is life after death in a way, if only because, if we have offspring, we pass on our genes to future generations. Otherwise, this book continues to remain firmly concerned with life before death.

In our final years, though we inevitably grow wearier in body and mind, we need to keep doddery decrepitude at bay. With the help of an increasing number of life-enhancing medical and surgical advances, *The Trailblazer Generation* can still keep on running after the fun fundamentals of life.

Signposts to the Future

'I love everything that's old: old friends, old times, old manners, old wines …'

– Oliver Goldsmith

In the latter part of the nineteenth century when the then mayor of Boston was shown an exciting new invention, the telephone, he remarked, 'I can see the time coming when one of these will be in every city in the nation.' As recently as 1943, the then Chairman of IBM said that there was probably a world-wide market for not more than five computers. With those examples behind us, as a final rally let us look to the future. We recognize what a dangerous business that can be, but we can still try.

What can those who are two or three decades younger than us expect to experience? Hopefully the walls of prejudice will have been further eroded and the institutionalized retirement of the elderly will have greatly diminished. As older people become an ever larger segment of the populations of all of the western world, negative attitudes to ageing will largely have disappeared. Treating the elderly as some sort of homogeneous group to be discriminated against will be totally outlawed. Instead our increased longevity will be widely seen as a magnificent achievement. Disengagement from the wider world by the elderly will be replaced by engagement, through maintaining the values we enjoyed in the past as well as building new activity patterns for the future. The population will be encouraged to think of their whole lifespan in a much wider perspective than prevails even today. They will retain much greater power to shape their own environment.

A new wave of *The Trailblazer Generation* will build on the huge advantages that we have already gained. The view from the top of their hill will be even better than the one we have experienced. They will continue to bank much of the nation's finances. They will hold onto public and private sector power for longer. They will have the experience and health to wield it well. But all the physical frailties of age will not be conquered for a long time yet and growing old will never suit the weak. The biological clocks will continue to tick, but the longevity of an increasing number of individuals will prove that it's better to be eighty years young than forty years old.

The percentage of the population that is ageing will always remain at one hundred percent. The Age Quake will continue to be a massive politico-social issue for the rich world throughout the first half of the twenty-first century. As the populations of almost all these developed nations continue to grow older, many practical things will be forced to change. Spring will come later and what was the winter of our lives will become their harvest time. Tomorrow's *Trailblazer Generation* will have little in common with today's new middle-aged, just as we lack similarities with those of a mere fifty years ago. Countries will be forced to redefine the balance of the generations as the once elderly, freed from a linear descent into traditional retirement, retain for much longer their hold as global leaders and entrepreneurs. They will live and work easily, well into their eighties and nineties.

Before plunging any further into that future, let's speculate that if someone from ancient Rome had come back from the dead in late Victorian times, little would have surprised him, except perhaps for steam trains and iron ships. With very little instruction he would have been able to cope with life. If, however, someone from a hundred, or even fifty years ago, were to emerge today, he would be completely lost amid the vast array of modern technology. The same will surely be true if we were in some way to venture into a future as little as twenty or thirty years ahead. We simply do not know what scientific and biological successes and tragedies lie ahead of us. But as predictions of life expectancy over that same period suggest that a hundred may become commonplace and a hundred and twenty not exceptional, given the exciting developments that are bound to delay future body-cell deterioration, we have to assume that there will be a total re-planning of all aspects of western society's intergenerational equity and fairness.

In financial terms our wage-earning lives will have to extend quite dramatically, to earn enough to live on after we stop. Our career structures will need rethinking in their entirety. We will use ourselves in better ways for longer, merging our abilities and our improved physiques with what society has to gain from us. That society will get used to retraining sixty- or seventy-year-olds into totally new professions or activities, so that they can continue to pay their way. And that's not so fanciful when we think of some of the startling career switches that people of late age make even today.

The pace and rhythm of life will also change. No longer will people be switched off at any set age, provided that they continue to be productive. The older a person is, the more their wisdom and experience will be properly recognized. Seventy will no longer be branded as old because most of the physical and psychological barriers that categorize those years will have disappeared. Eighty-year-olds, when being evaluated by others, will perhaps be told that they may reach their full potential in another decade or so!

Except for people in highly specialized professions, the 'job for life' which once dominated our careerist thinking will be dead in a decade. But as of today, a large proportion of the young will still be required to choose a career between the ages of sixteen and eighteen when they have not the slightest idea what they are letting themselves in for. They'll be presented with life's options when they are far less than a quarter of the way through it. Only a tiny fraction of them may still feel 'called', or know where their true interests might lie. As much as eighty percent of these young people's lives will still lie ahead of them. So why should they opt for only one career chosen in their adolescent years? All that will spark further change.

What has all this futurology got to do with *The Trailblazer Generation* of today? Answer: a great deal. We are constantly breaking into new territory. We know we can retrain. We too can pick up a new career as a carer, teacher or plumber. It's happening all over the place. Look again at how many of these senior public servants, still forcefully retired at a mandatory sixty, go off with their titles and make fortunes for themselves with new careers in business, in finance, or academia. But it should not just be individuals from these top echelons that achieve these benefits. How much the state school system could, for example, be improved by employing many more mature citizens instead of only young graduates, many of whom escape into new professions pretty soon in any case. With some retraining, many people of any age could teach timeless subjects such as English, literature, history, languages and the arts. Or, dare we say it, good citizenship.

Let's have a huge rethink. Let's not emulate the immediate past. This new encircling environment for the ageing will not be artificial like some horrendous Zimmer Olympics. Yet there are always dangers in having everything and still remaining inspired. Like a spoilt child, if we say, 'I want it now!' and our demand is immediately fulfilled, why do we bother striving for more? Everything has a sell-by date. New gimmicks fill the shelves. We in the rich world have enough of everything. Are we not satiated, even bored by excess? The answer is that with consumerism rampant, non-stop novelty will always create in us a desire for things we didn't know we wanted. At the moment we trade up to better cars, houses, computers, clothes, soaps and dog food. In future other un-thought-of things will continue to entice the desires of *The Trailblazer Generation.*

So many commercial strategies will have to change to cater to the growth and riches of the grey market. At the moment, even experienced marketers fail to recognize that people of our age do continue buying the new. It's we who, for example, spend most money on toys … for our grandchildren. We are also far more likely to purchase service items like financial, security, and home delivery products. Or we buy experiences, changing our homes for ones in warmer climates, or booking holidays rather than purchasing domestic items with which our houses are already full. It has taken a lot of travel companies a long time to discover that that elderly don't just want to sit by the swimming pool or pavement café and watch the world go by. We want adrenalin-filled adventure and experiences that we never had the leisure time to pursue in the past. They are at last beginning to recognize where the real money is stored.

In the advertising profession, young directors still largely ignore those of us who have far more disposable income than most people of their age. Or they treat us with golden oldie derision. They still believe that the young set all the trends and that older age groups don't follow suit. We don't change our minds as much maybe, but all that is going through a time mincer right now. We are fuddy-duddies no longer, and agencies will have to hire people who know where we big spenders are hiding. The little advertising that is presently directed at us is usually seen as patronizing or shallow, which is why so few of us relate to it. Do they really still believe that older consumers never change their brand loyalties?

On television, the elderly are currently used in advertising to sell medical insurance and stair lifts. But things are changing there as well. One lady hit the headlines recently. She is a wrinkled ninety-six-year-old great grandmother, whom an enlightened toiletry manufacturer used in one of their advertising campaigns. They should have done it years ago. At last we are beginning to have some recognition for our wrinkles; they have been hard-earned. Advertisers are starting to tell us what we have known for decades: that it's all about looking good *for* our age, rather than trying to look younger. It's a clever concept that is beginning to catch on since it challenges ageist concepts of what beauty is all about. There are other small signs of progress. Bookings of older models, known in the trade as 'classics', are also growing, as those who select and choose the relevant faces come to realize that looks are only a small part of attraction. It's the character of the face, the visual potential, the inner pride, the facial maturity, which tantalizes. Where do we see that in the faces of those physically perfect stick-insects who grace the covers of contemporary fashion magazines?

Many other aspects of our environment will continue to change quite dramatically. The designs of houses, public buildings, street signs and furniture, cars and other forms of transport, are gradually being adapted to meet the requirements of an ageing but still highly active population. But much more attention needs to be given to the little things of life. The wider introduction of easily controlled locks, door handles, taps, heating control panels and telephones, is becoming more common. But ways of opening difficult packages, designing readable labels and instruction booklets, easier cleaning and washing practices and so on, need to become equally commonplace. Devices which already exist to help the visually impaired or the hard of hearing, must become universal, along with brighter lighting in public places and, above all, safer neighbourhoods in which to live. There are many other things that will have to change too. The attitude that 'there's nothing I want to watch on TV', will be altered by more television channels being provided solely for the mature, along with the introduction of softer music and commentators speaking more clearly. And restaurant menus will be in much larger type!

General de Gaulle, as we mentioned earlier, famously wrote that the secret of success in government was not to let men grow old in their jobs. Perhaps so, but they can still contribute greatly by moving to other walks of life. The prospects for *The Trailblazer Generation* will be greatly assisted by other things that will change in society generally. We've already entered an era where work and play has merged because of home-based working practices brought about by modern computer technology. This concept of New Leisure will offer us all time for study, for reading, for self-expression, for looking after our bodies as part and parcel of a richer, better educated lifestyle. From the glorified excitement of sexy youth, there will be an ascending, rather than a descending, slope. The old will become more bold, exciting, and remain full of passion. That nasty word, gerontophobia, will be outlawed. Social exclusion and serious ill-health will become rarer and rarer, though physical and financial limitations will always be present.

Negative factors always march hand in hand with progress. In the not too distant past, it was predicted that, with robots and other aspects of modern technology, more and more people, particularly artisans, manual workers, and others in low-skill, repetitive occupations, would have work for no more than a couple of hours a day. This is already happening, leading to many people, in this freed-up time, becoming voyeurs of other people's lives. Any generation with too much time on its hands, does little for itself. As a substitute, more and more people spend their days watching other people doing things, by way of reality TV shows, internet porn, or endless games of manufactured football, with players, like the gladiators of old, bought from the third world or the decaying remains of the old Soviet Union. It's not just the elderly who have turned to living such second-hand lives.

On the upside, with the help of modern technology, the physical constraints that come with age will be further eroded. A twenty-year-old and an eighty-year-old, working at identical laptops, won't need to call on different energy resources from their respective bodies. Technologically adept senior citizens, less challenged by failing physical strength, will, as a result, be far more able to remain in work for decades longer than they do today. As VCRs have become outdated, on our way we can bin all those fables about anyone over fifty not being able to operate them. There's nothing new in all that. It is a true story that back in the 1950s, in some areas of Britain, telephones were not installed in a lot of old people's homes because 'they would not know how to use them'. Or there's the notorious bank which only recently told a friend who wanted to check his account on the internet that, because he was over sixty-five, they weren't sure whether someone of his age could cope!

If, in future, physical health no longer discriminates so much between the age groups, this could lead to there being less of a cultural divide between them. Given that we all have access to the same IT sources, we may begin to develop more similar tastes and outlooks on life. As massive corporate hierarchies and offices to which millions presently commute, disappear, we will be more able to set our own agendas and timetables to suit ourselves. It is an exciting prospect.

The Duke of Edinburgh, in a speech in the City of London in 2001, said, 'I can only assume that it is largely due to the accumulation of toasts to my health over the years, that I am still enjoying a fairly satisfactory state of health, and have reached such an unexpectedly great age.' It will take more than that to define our future health and prosperity. But great moments of our lives will still lie ahead. Younger generations are well known to be lazy about using their votes, so age should begin to set much more of the political agenda, particularly in deciding the distribution of our national resources. This will mean setting up more political movements, or wings within existing parties, to promote interests that are presently ignored. Younger political leaders are going to have to listen carefully to our concerns, not just about pensions, but about local tax rates, security, street crime, and medical and insurance matters.

Remember Disraeli, Gladstone, Churchill, not just because they added gravitas to the governance of the country, but because, back then, wisdom was considered to be born of experience rather than of opportunism. Skill, with age, can still be moved from one post to another with great effect. Good army generals can hold authority in other fields, as can lawyers, bankers and business tycoons, when given the right opportunity. Experience in pulling together boards of non-executive directors for commercial companies, has demonstrated that adding the skills of *The Trailblazer Generation* from outside the immediate area of a firm's activities, adds the greatest worth. Let us create more political and industrial gerontocracies. OK, by so doing the young will have to wait to step into our shoes, but they can benefit by taking up more quality time until they come to replace us. They can learn to become part and parcel of a future society where work and leisure are shared more equally across the generations.

No one worships the setting sun. *The Trailblazer Generation* in Western Europe and elsewhere is going to have to keep rethinking its place in society. It has much to learn from its American counterparts. We also need to enlist the help of the media if we want to gain more control of these agendas. Editors of newspapers continually create gods and devils, be they princes, footballers, politicians or pop stars. They act like the priests of yesteryear, building them up, having the populace worship them, and then, when they tire of them, or they no longer sell newspapers, they ritually slaughter them. Capturing headlines and the language to back them up is what our anti-ageist campaign must be all about. We must all become spin-doctors to sell our case.

Success in life can be compared to a baboon climbing a pole: the higher it gets, the less its appealing features stand out. To a very great extent, the length of our lives lies in how we present ourselves. Aches and

'When grace is joined with wrinkles, it is adorable. There is an unspeakable dawn in happy old age.'
– Victor Hugo

pains will not disappear for decades yet, but they are and will continue to be ameliorated with more new drugs and treatments. Keeping fit for as long as we can will become an automatic part of all future lifestyles. We all want to remain vigorous and alive. The declining nature of our bodies, from liver spots on skin, to hair loss, to sagging breasts and male reproductive organs, will be further revitalised. With an increasing number of bits replaced, we will be born anew. Older can and will be beautiful. We will be capable of remaining sensual until the end of our days.

To summarize, past perceptions that active, useful, life largely concluded on the day we retired from the rat race, are all being consigned to history. We, *The Trailblazer Generation,* have to help break that derelict mould, kick-starting the re-branding of the older age brand, and re-generaging as the new middle-aged. We're not living on borrowed time but as an ever healthier, wealthier, and more experienced age group. We demand and deserve a present and a future full of many more opportunities. Three score and keep scoring by us in these our *Freedom Years*, is what it's all about.

Two little words waken the sleepiest of audiences at the end of a lecture or talk. The same two words pop up now. They are 'In conclusion…' In conclusion, with the help of rapid advances in medical science, loss of mental capacity will be stemmed, and our intellectual and physical acuity will remain undimmed for many more years than at present. The superior knowledge and experience of age will more than offset the negative factors of ageing. We are all linked through time and our bodies will continue to act as the survival system for our genes. They will see us into the hereafter. In the meantime, we old dogs must use our *Freedom Years* to learn many new tricks.

Note from the Author and Publishers

Further editions of this book are planned. If any reader has advice supplementing or contrary to the material contained in this book, and would like to have it considered for inclusion in a future edition, the author would be delighted to hear from them. Any such contribution used will of course be fully acknowledged.